America's
Spiritual
Recovery

America's
Spiritual
Recovery

EDWARD L. R. ELSON

Introduction by
J. EDGAR HOOVER

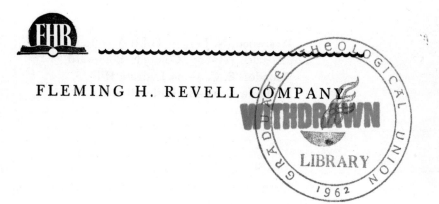

FLEMING H. REVELL COMPANY

Printed in the United States of America

Library of Congress Catalog Card Number: 53:10969

Westwood, N. J.—316 Third Avenue
Los Angeles 41—2173 Colorado Boulevard
London E. C. 4—29 Ludgate Hill
Glasgow C. 2—229 Bothwell Street

To

DWIGHT DAVID EISENHOWER

President of The United States of America

who

by personal example and public utterance

is giving testimony to

the reality of America's spiritual foundations

Contents

Introduction

~~~~~~

We are living in one of history's most difficult periods, and in an hour of widespread disruption, confusion, diversion and aggression. Temporary expedients, occasioned by the necessities of the times, have too frequently diverted our attention from time-honored and essentially valuable fundamentals.

The most fundamental fact of all is that the spiritual forces which have motivated our nation in its periods of greatness have been too frequently forgotten; we can now see all too clearly the devastating effects of the resultant Secularism on our Christian way of life. The period when it was smart to "debunk" our traditions undermined inspiring customs and high standards of conduct. A rising emphasis on materialism caused a decline of "God-centered" deeds and thoughts. The American home became a place of transient, furtive living and ceased to be a school of moral and spiritual education. Wartime conditions separated families and uprooted homes, community resources were neglected, the public schools suffered from a shortage of teachers, law enforcement was handicapped, and we had an outbreak of lawlessness that was unparalleled in our national history.

Our record of law violation has become a national disgrace. Today, one out of every 16 persons in the United States has been arrested and fingerprinted, while one out of every 31 persons has been convicted of one or more violations of the law. One family out of every 19 was affected in some manner by crime last year. The enormity of the crime problem is reflected by the fact that for every dollar spent on education, one dollar and eighty-two cents is diverted to the cost of crime. For every dollar given to the churches of this nation, crime costs us ten dollars.

When spiritual guidance is at low ebb, moral principles are accordingly in a state of deterioration. Secularism advances in periods when men forget God. And it is in these periods that the godless tyranny of atheistic Communism has made its greatest inroads.

But there are hopeful signs for a better day. There was hope in the words of General Eisenhower when he bowed his head on Inaugural Day and asked in part, "Give us, we pray, the power to discern right from wrong and allow all our words and actions to be governed thereby and by the laws of *this* land." This humble prayer touched Americans from coast to coast. Here was hope manifested in a manner which inspired the hearts of countless millions. A President with such a deep religious sense and with such a sincere spiritual motivation, seeking to be guided by the right, sets an example for all the people.

The fact that the author of this book could dedicate his important account of America's spiritual recovery to President Eisenhower is in itself a significant sign of the times. Our President exemplifies this spiritual development—the kind Dr. Elson discusses in this volume with clarity, forthrightness, and with such persuasion. A realist, the author looks with optimism upon our spiritual future. By his adherence to the fundamentals of his faith, Dr. Elson is marked as one of the nation's great preachers, and the fact that he has not lost contact with the man on the street makes him a great pastor. He makes a real contribution because he speaks from a life of broad experience and a deep awareness of Christian values in our national life. A man of God, with deep spiritual discernment, Dr. Elson lives his religion. To come under the influence of his personality is in itself inspiring.

J. EDGAR HOOVER

America's
Spiritual
Recovery

∿∿∿∿∿∿∿∿∿∿∿∿∿∿∿∿∿∿∿∿∿∿∿∿∿∿∿∿∿∿∿∿∿

CHAPTER I

The Moral Lapse

Old soldiers never die——and they never stop talking about their campaigns.

On the campus of one of our great American universities, a young man limped up and sat beside me in a malted milk bar. Observing from the button on his coat lapel that he was a World War II veteran, I asked the name of the outfit with which he had fought, and how he had acquired his limp. He replied that he had led an infantry section on patrol during the battle of the Colmar Pocket the day he got that limp; he also gathered in a fine assortment of bayonet and machine-gun wounds. He remarked, casually, that every man in his section had been killed or wounded.

It just happened that I had served in the same campaign; naturally, although we had never met up to that moment, we at once became good friends. He began to talk. He told me that he had spent long months in hospitals and convalescent institutions, fighting his way back to health. Now he was at his old university again, trying to pull together the broken threads of his life, and completing the education so abruptly interrupted by the War.

Of course, eventually I asked him how it was going with him at the university, and he gave me an answer that I shall never forget: "We have magnificent buildings here. We have splendid libraries and well-equipped laboratories. We have almost luxurious living-quarters. We have professors who know their subjects—*but they do not know the world.*"

It wasn't a criticism of "the cloistered, college mind"; he did not mean to say that his professors were ignorant men. For these men, as specialists in their particular fields, he had the greatest respect. But this soldier had "been to hell and back" in the few short years of his young life, and consequently he looked out upon the world through eyes quite different from those of his instructors. The world as viewed from the relatively insulated academic community of the university and the world of mingled battle and death and courageous gayety which had been this youth's were not the same world, by any stretch of the imagination.

Later that afternoon, on the same campus, I was trying to hold my own in one of those delightful question-and-answer sessions with a group of students. One of the co-eds looked at me blandly and asked, "Do you know what we talk about when we are alone?" I had some ideas about that, but, of course—for the purposes of the occasion—I pleaded innocence. She enlightened me: "We talk about whether we ought to be the mothers of children in this kind of brutal world, or whether we should refuse to give them birth and send them out meekly to die in another war." You don't answer that one hastily. I thought it over for a while before I replied, and I am not too sure, even yet, that my reply was worth very much.

Or here is a paratrooper who says to me, "I know eighteen ways to kill a man—twelve of them silently!" That is a notable achievement for a warrior, but it represents a difficult problem of adjustment for a soldier who has to come back and settle down in the days and ways of peace.

If the truth be told, it is probable that youths of this age, mature in thought and old in experience and flexible in outlook, have made a better job of that adjustment than we made in the days of *our* youth. They have more readily accommodated themselves to the pressures and forces of our post-war world than have their elders. But their attitudes are of genuine importance: disturbing as those attitudes are to the older generation, they often reflect pitilessly the moral ambiguities of our day.

It is an axiom of history that every war is followed by a moral sag. The greater the war, the greater the sag. And any man with any power of perception at all knows that we have been living, for quite some time, in a period of real moral sag and deterioration.

For instance, according to one of my parishioners, Mr.

17

J. Edgar Hoover, chief of the F.B.I., there occurred in 1953 (the latest year for which authentic figures are available) one major crime every 14.6 seconds. In this brief twelve-month period we find one burglary every 1.1 minutes, one robbery every 8.3 minutes, one larceny every 24.9 seconds, one rape every 29.4 minutes, one aggravated assault every 5.7 minutes, one automobile theft every 2.3 minutes, and one felonious homicide every 41 minutes! Think it over at your leisure! Every twenty-four hours, during that one year, there occurred thirty-five murders, forty-nine cases of rape and two hundred and fifty-four cases of aggravated assault.

And crime is only one of our problems.

There is also money. Everywhere there is a fatal indifference to the moral implications of money. The primary ambition of a vast host of modern people seems to be to get rich and get rich quick—to achieve wealth for its own sake by whatever method or methods are fast and effective. The veteran returning from the wars, seeing the financial success of the specialist or the "4-F" youth who stayed at home, proceeds in the mood of the day to "make up for lost time"—to square the account, and to "get his" while the getting is good.

As Americans we have developed a kow-towing admiration for the tycoons of business and the captains of industry; their success is one evidence of that enviable American freedom under which a man can rise to the heights. Of course, it might be good for us to stop to determine just how fine these "heights" are, but that opportunity to reach the peaks from a lowly start is still a basic concept and cornerstone in our society. And secretly, if not openly, almost every American aspires to improve his economic lot. The opportunity for financial betterment has been one of the attractions of the New World for people fleeing the more confining cultures of the Old World. As one rhymester puts it:

> France has her lily,
> England has her rose;
> Ireland has her shamrock
> As everybody knows.
>
> Scotland has her thistle
> On every downy hill.
> But the emblem of America
> Is the one-dollar bill.

Or so it was when the dollar was still a dollar!

To acquire money and to hold it as a custodian of the Almighty may be a laudable aim and pursuit, and to employ wealth as a steward of God may be to exhibit one of the primary Christian qualities. But to seek wealth for its own ends is a one-way street: it leads directly to the destruction of the soul. It is, for example, a tragic moment when a man looks into the face of his pastor and says, "I have discovered that it no longer pays to be honest in business." It is a moment of peril for all of us when the chief ambition of any of us becomes that of merely making money, regardless of that higher admonition of the Catechism which

19

claims that "the chief end of man is to glorify God and enjoy Him forever."

Throughout our land there is an un-Christian and therefore an antisocial attitude toward marriage and the home. Sacred vows are being repudiated and infidelity is condoned. Have you read the Kinsey Report? The hasty marriages of World War II, contracted in the mood of tentativeness, are now producing a heart-rending procession to and through the divorce courts of this land of the "free." If the present trend continues, by 1960 we will annually have half as many divorces as we have marriages. Whatever your philosophy or morality, it is difficult to see how that will benefit democracy!

The lack of parental respect shown currently by the children of America is appalling evidence of our renunciation of authority, our disdain for orderly processes, and our rejection of established customs and standards. Too many of us have jettisoned our ideals, walked over our ancestors' decencies and trespassed on humanity's sacred and valuable conventions. Perhaps some of those conventions may be outworn, but the trouble with us is that we do not stop to separate the outworn from the usable; we trample them down together. Too many of us have said, with the cynics, "To hell with the Ten Commandments!"—and then wondered why we seem to be going to pieces on the moral front!

When morality drops, the cultural level also sags. Since the turn of the century, we Americans have learned how to jazz our music and syncopate our thinking, to philosophize with boogie-woogie and esthetically cavort with the jitterbug. We produce paintings which, at least to a layman, appear to be a nightmarish astigmatism and an idiotic blur. Is this because our befuddled minds and shallow spirits can produce nothing better? *Collier's Magazine* recently ran a page of pictures in the "finger-painting" school—a series of slap-happy "pictures" and asked a group of wise psychology "experts" to guess who had painted them. The "experts" were very sure that the pictures had been done by boys and girls aged 7 to 10; they even described the characteristics of the young artists as revealed in the paintings. Then you turned the page to see portraits of the actual artists: the actual artists were two chimpanzees from the Baltimore Zoo! How stupid can we get?

When we look at the entertainment which has fascinated us in these post-war years, we have another tragic commentary on the kind of people we have become. Judged by box-office receipts, nearly all the screen dramas and stage plays which have been most successful have had a deteriorating personality at their center. To name a few, there is *Streetcar Named Desire, Harvey, Death of a Salesman, Come Back, Little Sheba, Blythe Spirit,* and *Lady in the Dark.* Every one of these, entertainingly or with poignant pathos, depicts an abnormal personality.

The significance of such an observation lies not in what all this reveals about the writers of the plays. They are brilliant; they understand us. The tragic thing lies in what this mood and appetite for entertainment say about us as a people—that we are a generation most interested in dramas with a "screwball" or a "crackpot" as the "hero."

21

If it is true—and orthodox psychology says it is—that we appreciate a play in direct relationship to our imaginative capacity to project ourselves into the hero's rôle, then the implications of this observation are clear and ominous.

As a generation, we dope ourselves with amateur psychology. We buy up all the books of the peace-of-mind cults, pitifully confident that it is possible to have peace of mind in our kind of world. We follow preachers who hawk formulas for banishing worry and fear and tension while the prophets of God, with their painful judgments requiring repentance, go unheeded. We turn wistfully to "inspirational" speakers, and are left with a terrible emptiness and loneliness of soul and a desperation of spirit. Every once in a while we realize that we are renegades from our true natures.

To man today comes a tragic sense of failure—failure in living. We are brilliant but unhappy, clever but unstable, comfortable but comfortless; we own so much and possess so little. We are forlorn souls, groping and hungering and lost. Once again, as in the Garden of Eden, man is a fugitive from God and bereft of spiritual certitude.

Individual man seems to be giving way to mass man. Man, the individual, whose free spirit was rediscovered and espoused in the Reformation, is threatened by a composite man. Man, the individual—with an immortal individual soul—standing in solemn grandeur as a created being before the sovereign majesty of his Creator, is yielding everywhere to collectivized man.

For two-thirds of the world's population the most inti-

mate details of everyday life are controlled by forces outside the individual. It may be less overt and deliberate
here than in the East, yet this regimentation is becoming
increasingly characteristic of Western civilization. The motion picture dictates our styles and sometimes our morals.
The columnist provides us with premasticated ideas. Book
clubs select our reading. Our business is done with chain
stores and chain banks. We live under a dictatorship of
psychological pressure and social atmosphere. Wherever
you look, mass man is encroaching on individual man.

The life of Western man, once sustained and uplifted by
religion, is progressively secularized. Services to human
lives which had their inception in religious faith and which
for centuries were motivated by the religious spirit no
longer have specific relation to religion at all.

Take, for example, the services of healing. Although
efforts to heal the human body are being made almost
everywhere, and although medical services antedate the
Christian era, the Christian Church has been the chief
exponent of the ministry of healing for many centuries.
Hospitals, originally, were "hostels"—way stations or rest
centers where travelers, especially pilgrims to the Holy
Land, could stop for spiritual and physical rehabilitation.
In earliest times the doctors were monks and the nurses
were nuns. It was the love of Christ in action which made
hospitals out of hostels.

While we thank God for the devoted physicians and
nurses whose deepest motivation to heal men springs from
a higher love for God, and while we thank God for hospitals

permeated with the spirit of Christ, too many hospitals today have become vast, impersonal healing-factories, with little or no intimate reciprocity between patient and physician. A sick man occupying a room in a large building often becomes "the case in room 1506," or a figure on a chart studied by a scientist in objective detachment. He cannot hope to know the warmth of personal concern which his father or grandfather might have experienced in less pretentious surroundings; nor, indeed, can the specialist, writing orders and making assignments to assistants, know the satisfaction experienced by his professional ancestor as he undertook the healing of the whole man.

Today almost half of our hospital beds are occupied by the mentally ill. If he is very fortunate, the patient may encounter a Christian psychiatrist who will treat him as though he were both a spiritual and a physical being. If not so fortunate, he may be attended by a physician who denies the very existence of the "psyche"—the soul of the man. Thus the science which derives its name from that very word, "psyche" (the human soul), limits its attention to the neuro-physical aspects of the patient's malady.

Education has undergone a similar process. This field, which in the Christian era had for its purpose the knowledge of God and the transmission of truth about God, does not today proceed on the premise that there is a God in and above all the processes of the universe. From ancient times before Christianity there were learned men, and in antiquity there were schools of learning, but it is a simple fact of history that education in our present world is the product of the Christian Church. Every time we see an academic gown and hood we should be reminded that, originally, these were the costumes of learned monks. And nothing in the modern world gave such impetus to education as the Protestant Reformation. Yet education, once fostered by religion and with God at the center of every academic pursuit, now relegates religion to a single department of instruction and God, no longer necessary, is saluted but rarely consulted or obeyed.

The profession of the jurist, historically, has had deep religious associations. The objectives of the lawyer were to achieve justice under a God who was the ruler of a moral universe; the bar of justice, before which he pleaded was once the communion rail. Today the lawyer bows in deference to the judge, but probably neither he nor the others present in a modern court are aware that the bowing all began because there used to be a crucifix on the wall above the judge's head before which all men must do obeisance. There are many men of faith and piety in the legal profession today, but it may well be questioned whether the main purpose of the modern court is to achieve God's righteous judgment, and whether the chief end of those engaged in its processes is to "glorify God and enjoy Him forever."

The secularization of life is observable everywhere. In modern industry management is committed to skilled specialists, while the energies and skills of labor are in the custody of vocational experts—the professional labor leaders who negotiate in terms of the "big business" which they represent. Even with the great economic improvements which the system has produced, and the religious motivations of some leaders of both labor and management, it can hardly be said that the dominant motive here is the fulfillment of St. Paul's injunction, "Whatsoever ye do, do all to the glory of God."

If there is any one ritual that belongs to and in the church it is the funeral ritual. Death brings God close—and yet we seem to be doing our best to deny it! We have taken the funeral out of the church and put it in a neutral place called "the mortuary," and given the whole ritual over to a professional expert called "the mortician." We neglect the hymn in the service for "Beautiful Dreamer" and selections from a symphony! The symphony certainly has its place; as a lover of music, I appreciate that. But it seems to some of us to be as out of place in a funeral service as dancing would be at a baptismal service. It also seems to border on the irreverent to hold the last offices for the deceased in unconsecrated "parlors" (at a very substantial fee!) completely unrelated to the sanctuary of God where in life the deceased offered praise and thanksgiving to his Maker.

Thus, in a thousand ways, life, once motivated by deep religious convictions and disciplines, has become increasingly secularized.

Meanwhile there hangs over us the terrifying thought that man by his own devices and his own moral choices, in one colossal incineration, may reduce his civilization to a mere memory floating on a vast galvanized desert. Some time ago, a scientist writing in the *Saturday Review of Literature* portrayed himself, his family, his friends and his enemies as component parts of a brightly-colored cloud rapidly dispersing some fifty-thousand feet above the surface of the earth. It remained for a distinguished psychologist to point out that the significance of atomic devices is not to be found in the threat of physical death to come but rather in the revelation of the spiritual death that is already with us.

Clearly, the predicament of modern man is this—that his technological and scientific progress has so far exceeded his moral and spiritual development that it is to be doubted that man can any longer be trusted with his own devices and his own destiny. It is clear that the basic problems of our age are moral and spiritual. The issues of our time turn not so much on politics and economics as on the kind of men and women who live in this world. That is why the ministry of religion is the most important work of our generation, and why it must once again permeate all of life.

Now there stalks across the world a new, militant atheism. It has evangelistic passion and crusading vitality. Its youth parades across vast areas of the world singing:

> It's the final conflict.
> Let each man take his place.
> The International Party shall be the human race.
> We are changing the world,
> We are changing the world.
> The *"Internationale"*

This new evangelism has in it the smell of factory smoke and sweaty bodies, of grimy hands and the lust for bread and "a place in the sun." We do not like its evangelism. We reject its materialistic dialectic. We repudiate its atheism. We loathe the manner in which it attempts to fashion men. But to deny or avoid its challenge would be consummate folly. To the discerning mind the sweeping events and the collision of forces in our age make explicit God's judgment on the processes of history. As the Psalmist said long ago, "The judgments of the Lord are true and righteous altogether."

There is in us a haunting conviction that if we are to match these days, if we are to meet the colossal obligations which God in His providence has imposed on us as a people, then God Himself must invade us from the outside. We *must* have a fresh encounter with the living Lord of the Universe who alone can fashion us into a people we never yet have been, yet always have longed to be.

As Americans we are confronted with tremendous obligations. Following two World Wars and the repulsion of the Korean aggression, we have become the stewards of the greatest military victories in all history, and in large measure we are today the guides of this world's destiny. To a very great extent the future of the race depends on what we are and on what we do. We are mighty, but hesitant; strong, but cautious; powerful, but burdened with anxiety. We are good, but we are far from certain that we are good enough. We are great, but not quite sure that we are great enough.

28

Our desperate need is for something—or someone—to awaken us to the greatness already within us, and the still nobler greatness which we may attain.

But what—or who—shall do that?

CHAPTER II

~~~~~~

The New Awakening

Dark and discouraging as the picture has been in our country and in the world across the recent years, there are bright and encouraging lights to break the shadows. Someone has said, "It is sure to be dark if you shut your eyes," and that is particularly true of modern America and Americans. He who puts us on the road to spiritual, moral, and physical disaster without hope shuts his eyes to our better side. Sometimes it takes a visitor from abroad to see that, when we ourselves cannot.

We had such a visitor in our National Presbyterian Church, in Washington, D.C., not so long ago. He was a Belgian, one of a group of European Chiefs of Chaplains on tour in this country. They sat in a pew directly across the aisle from the President of the United States, and they were impressed with his simplicity and naturalness in worship. They also noticed that the only reference to his presence in the sanctuary that day was a footnote on the Order of Service, asking the congregation to remain standing until the President had left the church.

To better understand our people these Chaplains had visited our large cities, observing our industrial and business centers; they had also visited a number of our small towns and rural areas, studying that spirit in America which can be found only in such places. They had been honored guests at military installations and church asemblies; they had conferred with religious, educational and political leaders. This was their last church service in the United States, and they were lavish with their praise. The chaplain from Belgium summed up the impressions of the group in a vivid speech. They were carrying away, he said, three indelible impressions which had transformed their outlook on our country:

First, they had found Americans to be a very *friendly* people. Wherever they went, on trains, in hotels, in church, in the army camps, they had found "an infectious friendliness that is unforgettable."

Second, they had found us a *democratic* people. They saw here a democracy they had never seen elsewhere. They saw less class consciousness, and a natural intermingling of all groups. They recognized people of many different racial, cultural and religious backgrounds, but they still saw us as a people forged into one body, remarkable for its absence of fear, its gay abandon to the job of living, and with a most

31

enviable freedom of action and expression. They heard some very funny and some very ridiculous things, but they also had heard some very serious and good things and words. Most Americans, they observed, read books, listen to the radio, or watch TV. We seem to have confidence in ourselves and a respect for others. Democracy, said the Belgian, is not only discussed in America; it is practiced.

Third—and this was the most important of all—they discovered that Americans are at heart a deeply religious people, and that their religious institutions exercise a subtle, persuasive influence in the life of the nation. They found churches open seven days a week, with crowded schedules of worship services, club meetings, missionary programs and multiple service projects; these were something to write home about, and they wrote home! Wherever they went, on any day of the week, the churches were thriving. When they attended a church service, particularly in the cities, they found themselves part of a congregation which habitually crowded the facilities available for worship.

These were the revelations of an America of which they had never dreamed. Perhaps a native American critic will report it differently; I am saying only that these men, looking at it from a stranger's unprejudiced standpoint, reported it so. Perhaps we natives are in the position of the man who couldn't see the forest for the trees.

Recently a member of the British Parliament, an active Anglican and a dedicated statesman, visited us. His most profound impression, he told me, was of our religious vitality. He had visited churches of all denominations, listened to able preachers and uplifting music, studied our programs of religious education, watched laymen in action, visited several national church conventions, and on one particular Sunday had been obliged to "queue up" at two churches before he could be seated for the morning service.

The truth of the matter is that no one can understand the United States except in terms of religion. America began in a spiritual quest. We achieved national existence by way of spiritual emancipation. We have survived because we are a religious people. When Americans act any other way than as a religious people they are not truly themselves. That is why some of our people, while traveling or residing abroad, seem ridiculous! By abandoning their natural ways and assuming an artificial sophistication, they are "out of character," and their portrayal of the American is a betrayal of their birthright and an insult to their heritage.

There have been intermittent periods of religious renaissance in our past, but we are living today in what probably is destined to be the greatest religious awakening in the history of our nation. There is convincing evidence that in the present epoch we are experiencing a moral resurgence and spiritual awakening of national proportions. The evidence is both overt and covert, but its total impact is not to be denied.

Many explanations are advanced for this religious renaissance. Some assert that it is the result of fear: fear of the

33

Communists, or fear of extinction in an atomic war. Others suggest that it results from the supposed failures of the United Nations and the intransigence of the Russians. By some it is believed to arise out of an inexperience in world politics on the one hand and the new obligation of world leadership on the other. The theologians conclude that it is the result of a shallow thinking and ambiguous faith with which we have become impatient, and with which we *must* be done.

Still others hold that this return to religion is the result of deep-seated sin in human life, a feeling of human inadequacy, a loneliness of soul, and an unfilled hunger for God.

No one of these explanations is sufficient in itself. The factors which have precipitated the revival are many and varied and complicated. What is indisputable is that we are living in a new age of faith.

A study made by Father Paul Bussard, editor of the *Catholic Digest,* as reported by The Associated Press, concludes that "the average American today believes in God, considers religion very important, attends church at least twice a month and thinks he'll go to heaven when he dies." In this survey, which is believed to be one of the most comprehensive surveys of religious beliefs and practices in the United States ever made, Father Bussard reports that ninety-nine per cent of Americans believe there is a God and that seventy-seven per cent think the soul lives on after death, seventy-five per cent of all American adults consider religion "very important," and twenty per cent say it is "fairly important," which suggests that in America religion is one of the most significant factors in the lives of American individuals.

Church membership has been steadily increasing in recent years. Six out of every ten Americans formally belong to a church—the largest ratio in the country's history. The actual adult church membership is about eighty-five million. It may be true that many are only nominal church members; it may also be true that of the non-member portion of the population a great many believers could be found who have not validated their faith by membership in any church.

Almost everywhere church attendance is sustained at a high level. Not only at seasonal religious festivals, or during the annual extended periods devoted to penitence and prayer, but on Sundays and weekdays throughout the entire year attendance has been unprecedented at the services of praise and thanksgiving, in which the Word is preached and the sacraments celebrated.

To provide for growing churches with expanding programs, a vast church building program has become a national necessity. During the War, when only emergency building was permissible, the United States Army Engineers became the largest builders of churches in the history of the world for a similar period. During the same period, and during the years immediately following the war, millions of Americans changed residences, not only once but some of them many times. Many moved hundreds, even thousands of miles from their earlier homes; it was the greatest population shift of the century. The growth of many existing communities was greatly accelerated. New towns and cities came into being with a fantastic suddenness. Organized religion tried to keep pace with the movement, but always lagged behind. Now the churches are endeavoring to establish themselves wherever Americans live—in the country, in older towns, and in new metropolitan centers.

Dependable and up-to-date statistics on church construction are difficult to procure. According to *Newsweek* (July 20, 1953), estimates indicate that by 1955 the Roman Catholic church alone will, over a ten-year period, have spent ten *billion* dollars on churches and parochial schools. In 1951, some $452,000,000 worth of new church buildings were erected. In 1953 that figure was exceeded. It has been estimated that at least $1,700,000,000 worth of new churches have been erected by Protestants since 1945, and who knows how much more is now on the drawing boards of the ecclesiastical architects? The end is not yet in sight.

To implement the church construction programs, professional money-raising firms have increased in number and in volume of business. Despite high prices, high taxes, the universal appeal of new mechanical contrivances, and the rising costs of maintaining a church program, the building of new churches is one of the most impressive characteristics of the American landscape today.

Mass evangelism, which only a few years ago was thought by many to be a bit outmoded, is now reappearing with dynamic impact. By brilliant salesmanship, moving preaching, and capable management, the techniques of the hippodrome and the amphitheater are once again winning men and women and youth to Christ. What is even more significant is that those who find God by this method and resolve to live a new life are being carefully integrated into the churches by the most skillful educational evangelism yet developed by professional evangelists. All of this is happening at a time when evangelism by personal visitation and the continuous processes of Christian education have attained their greatest effectiveness.

There are many earnest, sincere, and hard-working men offering their energies as specialists in Christian evangelism. Several are commanding national attention, and their efforts are attended by phenomenal success.

God speaks to each generation in its own terms, through contemporary personalities and the language of the day. Thus, in this television age of glamour and drama, He has placed His hand on three winsome personalities of extraordinary personal appeal. One of them is Billy Graham. This Southern Baptist, with intense fervor, warmhearted oratory, and a machine-gun delivery, crusades against sin in places high and low. Youthful, virile, incisive, earnest, his messages are constructed on the pattern of the old-fashioned evangelist, yet they are as modern in expression and application as the morning breeze. Attacking sin that is both personal and social, Billy preaches for verdicts and gets them. For several years he has been conducting interdenominational campaigns in great metropolitan centers; these campaigns have won the attention of thousands of people. Wherever he goes with his capable

37

associates, the Christian cause dominates the news. Using the largest available auditorium, his crusades (which cover a period of four or five weeks) begin modestly but move with increasing intensity until the very end, which is uniformly the most dramatic and frequently the most penetrating part of the entire campaign. Demands for his service are many times greater than the possibility of meeting them. He steadfastly declines to enter on a major evangelistic effort without the co-operaion and encouragement of the principal churches of the community. He has created perhaps the most efficient system yet developed for integrating converts into the churches of their choice, thus conserving permanently both the convert and the spiritual impact of the crusade on the community. The auxiliary features, such as special meetings for clergy and for church officers, are unusually constructive.

Meanwhile, Billy produces a weekly radio program, known as "The Hour of Decision," which is carried into millions of homes. His television programs have brought his team and their message into many other homes. He has written several widely circulated books, and produced some evangelistic motion pictures of real merit. Last year he closed a campaign in Dallas, Texas, preaching to a congregation of 75,000 people in the Cotton Bowl. Still in his mid-thirties and continually growing in spiritual insight, Biblical knowledge, theological wisdom, and convincing expression, he has already proved himself one of God's chosen instruments for the redemption of the nation.

Equal in strength and stature, with solid theological content and superior preaching talent, another young man has captured America's attention. Charles Templeton, a personal friend of Billy Graham's, has the quiet persuasiveness of the master salesman, combined with homiletic talent and intellectual substance, and an almost uncanny comprehension of the stresses and strains of modern life. Few who come under the influence of Charles Templeton leave his services unmoved.

Possessed of a massive, athletic physique and a profile which would have won him fame on the stage, he is not what one usually pictures as "the ministerial type." Born and reared in a humble Canadian home, self-taught, Templeton began his early career as a sports cartoonist, and then heard the call of God to the ministry. Without benefit of theological training except for a correspondence course, supplemented by studies in public speaking, he practiced preaching in empty churches, talked into mirrors, and read continuously to compensate for his lack of formal education. With his small savings he leased an abandoned church building in Toronto and within two years had built a non-denominational congregation of several thousand people. As the result of a fire which destroyed this building, a new church edifice was constructed; within five years it was completely free of debt. Meanwhile, he had been on intermittent evangelistic tours. At the end of seven years, he felt the need of a more thorough theological education. Although he possessed no college degree, his intellectual maturity prompted Princeton Theological Seminary to admit him as a special student. Upon the com-

39

pletion of his seminary course, he was ordained a Presbyterian minister and appointed evangelist under the National Council of Churches which represents some thirty-five million Protestants. Because of the quality of his preaching, almost any pulpit in America is open to him. He is booked two years in advance for evangelistic services.

With the diagnostic skill of a great physician and expert psychiatrist, Charles Templeton gets close to people, describes their ills to them, and prescribes the remedy— Jesus Christ! He understands the Church and believes in the Church as the medium of God's spirit in the earth. He wants to work in and through the Church and to strengthen it.

As an evangelist, his impact on the cities he has visited has been immeasurable. In Evansville, Indiana, out of a population of 128,000 there was a total attendance of 91,000 in his meetings, over a period of two weeks. In Sydney, Nova Scotia, out of a population of 30,000 there was a congregation of 10,000 on his closing night. Of his visit to one American city, a public official said that "not in living memory has any event, secular or religious, so moved this community."

Writing about "Religion's Super Salesman," Edward Boyd described for *American Magazine* (August, 1953), his impressions of one of "Chuck" Templeton's sermons:

There was an unmistakable element of hope and optimism in all he said. Religion was no longer a solemn, formal, worn-out thing with the appeal of the graveyard. It was, on the contrary, happy, warm and vital. He presented it as a challenge and an exciting way of life. . . . At the risk of sounding sacrilegious, I would say that Chuck is to religion what Mickey Mantle is to baseball or Perry Como to his singing fans. He makes religion as enjoyable as these people make sports or music enjoyable.

There can be no question that this studious, growing young minister is a man of destiny in the church and the world.

Both Templeton and Graham live simple, quiet lives and have endeavored to remove the accusation of commercialization from evangelism. Both have eliminated the "love offering" for themselves, which was a custom of evangelists in the past. Both receive salaries—Templeton from the National Council of Churches, Graham from his own evangelistic corporation. Both men have already campaigned in Europe, and have plans for campaigns in the future.

Holding the television spotlight and a reputation for sensational conversions to Roman Catholicism is The Most Reverend Fulton J. Sheen. Loretta Young (a good Catholic herself) once called Bishop Sheen "The finest ham in the business," and she meant it as a compliment, and it is quite true. On TV Bishop Sheen has won a larger audience than Milton Berle or Bob Hope. The Videodex Report puts his audience at about 10,000,000, and DuMont officials say privately that it is even higher. He is easily the strongest letter-puller on TV; better than 8,000 letters come in from his audience every week. DuMont has some 5,000 requests per week for tickets to his broadcast, and can give out only

1,100. One little prayer book offered by the Bishop over the air brought requests for 640,000 copies, and his book, *Life Is Worth Living,* has gone well past the half-million mark and been on the nation's best-seller lists.

This audience of Bishop Sheen's is remarkable; it contains not only Roman Catholics, but Protestants and Jews and men and women of every conceivable turn of mind. It is probable that he has preached to more Protestants than any other Roman Catholic in history; there are perfectly good Methodists and Presbyterians who would not miss his broadcast for anything! Philosopher and theologian, brilliant preacher, and consummate stage artist, he has an uncanny understanding of the common man and a God-given ability to present profound truths and ideas in such plain and simple language that the humblest of men can understand. He draws on the resources of history and on his age-old theology to answer the questions and to cure the illnesses that trouble us today. He can talk to the philosopher and the mechanic in the same breath. He knows the past and he knows our age. His outlook has eternal dimensions. His appeal is to youth as well as to age, to the pagan as well as to the pious. When he appears, it is open season on atheists, pagans, the disillusioned, the heart sick and every variety of sinner. Yet the saints hear him gladly, pray for him, and give him their blessing.

So the mood of the day, the craving of men's hearts, the means of communication, and these providentially provided personalities, all converge at this point in history, attesting God's hand at work in today's world.

The momentum for the current spiritual awakening comes not only from the religious specialist but also from the layman. How so many strong laymen's movements got under way so quickly no one seems to know; they appear to have arisen almost spontaneously, certainly without benefit of clerical generation. In any case, the once latent energies of the laymen within the churches are now being efficiently organized and channeled through the religious institutions of our land.

In every major communion of Protestantism there are dynamic laymen's organizations, making necessary a recently established laymen's department in the National Council of Churches. Inspiring national and regional conventions are held, and all alert congregations have active laymen's councils. Leadership training conferences instruct laymen in ways to use millions of "man-hours" for God's glory. In many American cities Christian business men meet for a weekly breakfast, lunch or supper for fellowship and prayer and to draw outsiders into the circle of Christian believers, and spiritual retreats "for men only" are establishing the personal spiritual disciplines which make for victorious living. In everything pertaining to church—its worship, its evangelism, its Christian education and its social action—there are lay movements which really move men for the Kingdom of God.

That comparable organizations exist within the Roman Catholic and Jewish faiths is part of the accumulating evidence of the American resurgence in religion.

Separate from the Church, but supplementing and feed-

43

ing into its life, are such powerful organizations as Alcoholics Anonymous. This organization uses all the old techniques of the Church—confession, repentance, group fellowship, public testimony, and personal prayer—in new application and with amazing effectiveness.

World War I produced a "flapper-and-flask" generation, the effects of which are still evident. World War II produced a great moral sag, but it also has been a period in which men have been alerted to the need for God in their lives. For one thing, the military establishments provided for religion as no other nation in all history has provided for the spiritual needs of its military emissaries. Wherever Americans went in war they were accompanied by ministers of religion representing all phases of our religious culture. In permanent garrisons, simple but adequate churches were erected—sometimes more inspiring than the churches back home. Chaplains were supplied with the best religious field equipment ever developed. The qualifications for appointment (which involved factors of age, physical condition, professional training, temperamental and emotional fitness, and ecclesiastical status) guaranteed that man for man the chaplains would be equal to the average of their contemporaries among the American clergy. No one denomination could be said to have had an exclusive monopoly on all the strong chaplains, and there were just enough "duds" in each to prevent any sectarian boasting.

The stories of how our young military men encountered God and came to possess a living Christian experience during the War are too well known for repetition here.

What is not so well known is that during this period many young men were confronted *for the first time* with the call of God to the Church's ministry. Many men came closer to ministers of religion while in uniform than they had ever come in mufti. At one time during the war, the Army Chief of Chaplain's office had listed thousands of young men who had declared their intention to prepare for the ministry when the war was over.

The present pastor of a growing Lutheran church in Grand Rapids was the young soldier who drove my jeep through thousands of miles of combat. I knew a Baptist minister from the South as a private first class clerking in the chaplain's section of an army corps in Europe. One commanding general reports that every personal secretary who served him during the war became a Methodist minister. A graduate of West Point, wounded and retired as a colonel in his thirties, has just completed his theological education and been ordained to the Protestant Episcopal priesthood. A naval officer who resigned his commission in the regular service has recently completed seminary, been ordained a Presbyterian minister and commissioned a missionary to the Camerouns in Africa. These stories could be repeated a thousandfold.

These young men have crowded the divinity schools of the nation since the war and are conspicuous in the younger leadership of the Church today. It is the unanimous report of the presidents and deans of theological schools that this group of young spiritual leaders—war-conditioned, deeply consecrated and desperately in earnest

45

—are the best disciplined, the ablest scholars, and generally the most promising group of young clerics to complete seminary in half a century.

War can never be said to be good, but perhaps we may not be in error when we point out that one of the better by-products of this tragic era has been the general improvement in the religious leadership of our people. Taken together, the chaplains who served during the war and the young men who became ministers through the war are perhaps the most widely traveled, the most ecumenical in outlook, and the most human in understanding yet produced in America. Whatever else may be said about churchmen today, the conclusion will not seriously be challenged that when this group has been added to the already strong body of clergy, America will be in possession of the best spiritual leadership in her history.

Theological education shows the impact of an intensification of the religious spirit in America. Although there remains a shortage of ordained ministers in most of our religious bodies, the enrollment at divinity schools is the highest in our history. Given a few more years at the present rate of recruiting, the churches may be provided with not only the most competent but the largest corps of trained leaders it has ever known.

With the expansion of the churches and the increased enrollment of candidates for church vocations, the theological faculties have been improved. Never before have we had so many excellent institutions or such able instructors in church vocations. Once, young American theological students went to European educational centers for supplemental graduate study; some still go abroad, but more for the European touch than because European schools are superior. Great theologians and great teachers of religious subjects have been developed here. Moreover, in recent years many of the leading theologians of Europe have joined the faculties of American institutions. Student travel to other lands is somewhat reversed by the presence of these foreigners in American divinity schools.

This has all the more meaning when we understand that we are living in a period in history remarkable for its great theologians. The list of great Christian historians, theologians, philosophers, and apologists is too long for entry here, but any well-informed observer will tell you that the present age is characterized by the presence of as great Christian thinkers as have appeared in several centuries.

The colleges and universities show signs of the awakening among undergraduates. Everywhere there is a new earnestness and seriousness on the part of students. To be sure, secularism is quite general and some cynicism remains. Perhaps the equivalent of the old Student Volunteer Movement with its slogan, "The Evangelization of the World in this Generation," has not yet appeared; nevertheless, widespread groups dedicated to God are coming together for prayer and study. Some belong to the "Fellowship of the Yoke"—a disciplined group of young people whose symbol is "The Yoke of Christ" and whose purpose is to demonstrate the love of God in action. Other young

47

people participate in denominational campus programs or in various other student Christian movements.

Dr. Louis H. Evans, minister-at-large for the Presbyterian Church in the U.S.A., reports that he has found "a tremendous nostalgia for God on the campuses." Says he, "I've received fifty-three invitations in two months from universities; invitations have come, too, from teachers' institutes. In a single state I am to speak soon to 12,000 to 20,000 teachers, and other talks are scheduled for national conventions of school personnel. It is especially gratifying to fulfill these commissions, for I regard school people as the trustees of the nation."

Religion is gaining new acceptability on the campus. It is more than a leavening influence. It may soon be the dominant force among undergraduates everywhere.

Below the university level educators are groping to find some way in which to include religion in their curricula and to inculcate religious disciplines and attitudes in the students. The National Educational Association and the National Congress of Parents and Teachers are giving increasing attention to the place of religion in the development of life values, personal character, and democratic living. New devices for implementing religious education within the framework of American public education are being explored.

We have been considering the great awakening as seen within the church and education, but all this is not so immediately perceptible to the man in the street as is the American Legion's "Back to God" program or "Operation

48

Pray" sponsored by the Junior Chamber of Commerce, or the persistent religious accent in the service clubs. Perhaps a few are startled, when dining out to have handed to them in place of the usual cocktail menu, a card containing prayers to be said before the meal—prayers for Protestant, Catholic, and Jew. No one can escape the impact of religion through radio and television. So much a part of modern life has religion become that no modern radio or TV station could meet its audience demands without vital religious programs.

The "Good News" of the Gospel has also become newsworthy copy for the daily press. That religion is one of the liveliest topics of the time is indicated by the assignment by newspapers of some of their best talent to reporting religious news. It is significant that the attempted Congressional investigation of the clergy produced more copy and drew larger audiences than any Congressional hearing since the Hiss trial.

All the news magazines contain religious sections, edited by specialists in religious journalism. A generation ago the magazines carried an occasional religious feature; today no magazine would be up-to-date without a featured religious story in every issue. Such stories portray religious events and personalities with the same diligence and accuracy given to politics, science, art, and medicine. Not only is an occasional sermon "hot copy" for the daily press, but some sermons have appeared in their complete text in the more sophisticated weekly and monthly periodicals.

Religious periodicals have continued to grow, both in

49

number and in circulation. *Christian Herald* has a circulation of 378,000; *Presbyterian Life* has a circulation of 715,-000, and *Christian Advocate* reports 288,000. There has also been a marked improvement in the editorial content and in the format. Some of the most capable editors today are directing religious productions. The journals of the Church are becoming as modern as the age they serve.

Symptomatic of the spiritual craving of Americans is the vast sale of devotional handbooks. Guides to daily devotion and anthologies of spiritual readings are sold in large quantities, in the bookstores and on the news-stands as well as in the churches. Dr. Glenn Clark has circulated nearly 1¾ million of his devotional books and booklets; *Upper Room*, among the Methodists, has a circulation of 2,873,000, and *Secret Place*, an American Baptist devotional guide, reaches 420,000.

Weary of the sex-centered author, with his shallow plot and gutter emphasis, and a little fed up with the cheap "mystery" story, Americans are turning more and more to religious books. If the reports of the publishers mean anything at all, a revolution is under way here; if we are not undergoing a spiritual awakening in this country, then someone had better step forward quickly with some other sensible explanation of the unprecedented audience now being granted the authors of religious books by our people.

This trend started some years ago, and it snowballed. According to the Department of Commerce, the 1947 book volume was twice that of 1927, and nearly three and a half times that of 1937. But we need not go back to a 1947 report for evidence here; suppose we look at 1953. *Time* magazine for December 21, 1953, listed the best-sellers of the year. Number one on the fiction list was *The Robe*; that religious novel won first place on this best-seller list in 1943, and it has a record of 174 weeks on the list, on and off, ever since. (No other book ever written in America, we believe, can make that statement!) Third on the fiction list for 1953 was Thomas Costain's *The Silver Chalice*.

But it is when we look at the non-fiction best-sellers for the year, as reported in *Time*, that we feel the real impact of religious books. *Time* listed the six top sellers in non-fiction, and five of them were religious! Leading them all was the new *Revised Standard Version of the Bible*, with a record of over 2,000,000 copies sold during the year. Second was Norman Vincent Peale's *Power of Positive Thinking*, which did nearly as well as the top three fiction best-sellers put together! Third was *Angel Unaware*, by Dale Evans Rogers, with a record of 300,000 copies sold in one year. Dr. Kinsey's *Sexual Behaviour in the Human Female* ran fourth in the list, with something around 200,-000—a disappointing sale in spite of all-out promotion. *Life Is Worth Living*, by Bishop Fulton J. Sheen, ranked fifth, and Catherine Marshall's *A Man Called Peter* (120 weeks on the list, as we write) was in sixth place.

We may be wrong, but we believe that this has never happened before in the history of American publishing. When religion takes over in the field of best-sellers something is happening in the American mind!

Go back across the past decade, and study these lists. All

through the forties, Dr. E. Stanley Jones was enjoying an unprecedented sale of his devotional books; his *Abundant Living* sold more than 750,000. Dr. Harry Emerson Fosdick gave us his popular *On Being a Real Person* in 1942, and in 1949, *The Man From Nazareth*; and his three "meanings"—*The Meaning of Prayer*, *The Meaning of Faith*, and *The Meaning of Service* are still tremendously popular. Thomas Morton, a young Trappist intellectual, hit the list with his *Seven Storied Mountain* and *The Sign of Jonas*, describing his spiritual quest and life in a monastery. Catherine Marshall had her first best-seller in 1949 *Mr. Jones, Meet the Master*, which to date has sold 375,000 and that was a book of sermons, which are supposed not to be of much interest to the average reader!

Do you recall the startling popularity of *Peace of Mind*, by Rabbi Liebman, and *A Study of History* (a deeply religious book), by Arnold Toynbee? Who can forget those other books by the author of *The Robe—The Magnificent Obsession* and *The Green Light*? At one time, on the best-seller lists in the forties we find *The Greatest Story Ever Told*, by Fulton Oursler (a Roman Catholic), *The Nazarene*, by Sholem Asch (a Jew) and *The Robe*, by Lloyd Douglas (a Lutheran). Those three books all on the list at the same time say a great deal for the growing spiritual awareness of the American people, and for their growing tolerance and understanding. They seem not to care very much whether a book is written by a Roman Catholic, a Protestant, or a Jew, so long as it is (1) well written, (2) a sincere account of a sincere religious experience and (3) told in terms that the clerk as well as the theological professor can understand. We might keep in mind, too, that the old King James version of the Holy Bible has been a best-seller with an annual circulation of at least a million copies, year in and year out, longer than most of us can remember.

There is another, and all-important, stimulus behind our spiritual awakening: it is found in the inspiring leadership of the President of the United States. It may not be too much to say that through his personal conduct and expression he has become, in a very real sense, the focal point of a moral resurgence and spiritual awakening of national proportions.

Early in the morning of January 20, 1953, the man who was that day to be inaugurated the nation's thirty-fourth President entered a quiet Washington church. There, surrounded by his family and joined by his Cabinet and their families, he sought strength in prayer and in the Word of God for his overwhelming new responsibilities. All of us present at that service will forever believe that the power of the Holy Spirit moved in the earnest hearts gathered in God's house on that historic day. Former presidents had gone to church with their families for private prayer on Inauguration Day, but this service was made unique by the presence of members of the Cabinet and their families.

The company joined with General Eisenhower in singing the familiar hymn, "Our God, Our Help in Ages Past."

53

Among the Scripture lessons which he heard read was one containing the prayer of Solomon in I Kings 3:7-14:

And Solomon said, . . . O Lord, my God, thou hast made thy servant king instead of David my father: and I am but a little child: I know not how to go out or come in. And thy servant is in the midst of thy people which thou hast chosen, a great people, that cannot be numbered nor counted for multitude. Give therefore thy servant an understanding heart to judge thy people, that I may discern between good and bad: for who is able to judge this thy so great a people? And the speech pleased the Lord, . . . and God said unto him, Because thou hast asked this thing, . . . behold, I have done according to thy words: lo, I have given thee a wise and an understanding heart. . . . And if thou wilt walk in my ways, to keep my statutes and my commandments, as thy father David did walk, then I will lengthen thy days.

Prayers were offered for the nation, for all in authority, and for world peace; then the pastor offered the following petition:

Almighty God, who by Thy providence, through the voice of this people, hath summoned Thy servant, Dwight David Eisenhower, to the office of President of these United States, look with favor upon him in this solemn hour of dedication. Grant unto him now and henceforth health of body, serenity of soul, clarity of insight, soundness of judgment, a lofty moral courage, a sanctified stewardship of office, and a constant and confident faith in Thee. Keep him ever sensitive and obedient to Thy Spirit. Make him a channel of Thy grace and an instrument of Thy power upon this earth, that righteousness and truth, justice and honor may be promoted and upheld among the men and nations of this world. Let goodness and mercy follow him all the days of his life, that he may dwell in Thy house forever. Through Jesus Christ our Lord. Amen.

A period of silent prayer was concluded as we recited the Lord's Prayer and rose to sing the immortal words of the great hymn by Hugh T. Kerr:

God of our Life, through all the circling years, we trust in Thee;
In all the past, through all our hopes and fears, Thy hand
we see.
With each new day, when morning lifts the veil,
We own Thy mercies, Lord, which never fail.

God of the past, our times are in Thy hand; with us abide.
Lead us by faith to hope's true Promised Land; be Thou our
guide.
With Thee to bless, the darkness shines as light,
And faith's fair vision changes into sight.

God of the coming years, through paths un-known We follow
thee;
When we are strong, Lord leave us not a-lone; Our Refuge be.
Be Thou for us in life our Daily Bread,
Our heart's true Home when all our years have sped.

The Presbyterian Hymnal

In this mood, placing the destiny of the Nation in God's hands, the company received the benediction of the Lord and lingered for a moment in silent prayer. The nation's new leader, his wife at his side, rose quietly and left the church. In the mood of this service, and in fulfillment of a long-considered desire to include his Cabinet and the nation in a very personal act of dedication, he paused for a few quiet moments in his quarters at the Statler Hotel to strike off the words which have since come to be known as "my little prayer."

55

In the shadow of the Capitol dome Dwight David Eisenhower placed his hand on an old family Bible and took the oath of office as President of the United States. His first two acts as President were simple acts, but filled with enduring meaning. First, he stepped to the side of his wife and kissed her, symbolizing his personal devotion and the sacredness of the American home. Secondly, symbolizing the faith which pervades our national existence, he invited the throng before him and millions listening around the world to bow with him as he offered the prayer he had written just a little while before:

Almighty God, as we stand here at this moment, my future associates in the executive branch of the government join me in beseeching that Thou wilt make full and complete our dedication to the service of the people in this throng and their fellow citizens everywhere. Give us, we pray, the power to discern right from wrong, and allow all our words and actions to be governed thereby and by the laws of this land. Especially, we pray that our concern shall be for all the people, regardless of station, race, or calling. May co-operation be permitted and be the mutual aim of those who, under the concepts of our Constitution, hold to differing political faiths, so that all may work for the good of our beloved country and Thy glory. Amen.

This unexpected revelation of the deep spiritual quality of the new President lifted the entire ceremony to a high level and transformed all that followed thereafter. All that has transpired since then in the public life and spoken word of President Eisenhower has sprung likewise from this spiritual quality. Whatever else this President is remembered for, future generations will mark him as a President who from the highest seat in the land brought a new moral tone and spiritual virility into American life.

Before his election to the Presidency, General Eisenhower had frequently declared his concern for the recovery of America's religious foundations. Senator Frank Carlson of Kansas, his intimate friend, recalls that the President said to him at the dedication of a chapel at Kansas State College, while Eisenhower was still in the Army: "Frank, I don't believe our country will ever be the country that our forefathers had planned, and God has intended for us, unless we get back to fundamental spiritual principles."

Since his election his personal faith, grounded on the strict religious upbringing of his River Brethren parents, disciplined by Bible study and prayer, matured and modified with the passing of the years, has been evident in all he has undertaken. Twelve days after assuming office, he quietly validated his long-demonstrated Christian faith by becoming a communicant member of The National Presbyterian Church in Washington. Bearing the burdens of the heaviest office in the world, he regularly worships on Sunday in his own church and, when out of the city on week ends, he invariably attends some other church.

The example of President and Mrs. Eisenhower in church attendance once more highlights the "family pew" and makes a most valuable contribution to the re-establishment of habits of worship in the American home. The harried business man who must have his Sunday golf must now be somewhat troubled in conscience as he reflects on

57

the Sunday morning activity of the equally avid golfer in the White House.

President and Mrs. Eisenhower's attendance at church is having a far-reaching influence on the people. As an editorial in the Jacksonville, Florida, *Times-Union* pointed out on July 12, 1953:

There is something soul-stirring about Ike's church going, something that makes a person feel as if the President enters a sanctuary to gain strength, wisdom, and guidance from an All-seeing Power that resides above. . . . From the same source that Eisenhower finds divine guidance to steer a straight course over the uncharted waters that lie ahead, there is a new way of life for others who would follow the example of the White House and seek where it can be found, and ask where it can be given.

Being true to his own faith, Eisenhower inspires men of other faiths to greater zeal. A Roman Catholic, John J. O'Brien, in an article in the National Catholic magazine, *The Sign*, for August, 1953, declares that "the man who has brought spiritual values to the forefront of government more than at any time since the early years of the republic is President Dwight D. Eisenhower." Bishops and priests have spoken in gratitude for this leadership in a return to religion. American rabbis bear witness to the influence of the President's practices on the Jewish community.

It is not only in his habit of formal worship, but in his discipline of prayer that the President is a symbol of our contemporary religious renaissance. Several mornings after his inauguration, at a prayer-breakfast attended by Cabinet officers, members of the Congress, the Judiciary, business men and some religious leaders, President Eisenhower witnessed to the power and meaning of prayer in his life. He testified that prayer put him in touch with the Infinite and, by opening his mind and heart to God, he found Divine energies flowing through him with which he could undertake his duties and solve his problems. He drew on several instances in his own life which confirmed his abiding faith in prayer and commended to others the way of prayer.

In past years, Cabinet meetings were occasionally undertaken by invoking God's blessing. Today every Cabinet meeting opens with prayer, led either by a Cabinet member or offered silently by each man. Every meeting of importance at the White House is instituted with prayer, as for example, the Governors' Conference, at which the President's pastor led in prayer immediately preceding his address. It is not an exaggeration to say that the business which receives the attention of the President is surrounded with the atmosphere of prayer.

The President's emphasis has given a fresh masculinity to religion in general and to prayer in particular. Important educational assemblies and business meetings, heretofore negligent of spiritual values, are now introducing prayer into their deliberations. A member of a large corporation board wrote a letter to the author, saying that the chairman of the board had announced his intention of beginning every board meeting with prayer and that the writer was designated to pray at the next meeting. The letter closed with a plaintive inquiry: "What do I do now?"

This Presidential leadership has come at a time in American history when Americans are responsive to its promptings. What is important now is that this religious awakening be given every possible momentum in order that our total life may be saturated by the reality of God's presence and our nation be a citadel of spiritual strength to all mankind.

Americans are building churches and attending them, buying religious books and reading them, praying and preaching, giving to and serving their God, winning others and working for Him, and our youth is being alerted and dedicated to Him.

We are not perfect, but we have found a perfect Lord; we are not holy, but we have found a Holy God to worship; we are not without sin, but we have discovered where sins are forgiven; we are not spiritually completed, but we are growing in the things of the Spirit. If the revival continues, God may yet use us for the redemption of His world.

The tides of time have swept the nation to heights of moral excellency and spiritual power. There have been periods, too, of moral recession and spiritual timidity, and we are not yet completely free of these dangerous shoals, but the God who made us has not forsaken us. Somehow or other, Americans always get back to Him. The forces at work today make it clear that we are getting closer to Him than we have been for many a long year, and that spiritual recovery is all about us.

CHAPTER III

~~~~~~

Freedom Is Born of Faith

For Americans the practice of liberty is an every-day vocation. This is so true that its familiarity has bred, if not
contempt, a regrettable carelessness and lack of appreciation in John Doe, common citizen. John, right now, seems
not only to be taking this priceless possession without any
sense of gratitude whatever; he seems to be forgetting the
tremendous forces which brought him this freedom, and
their deep influence on our origin and development.

He forgets, for one thing, that the signing of his beloved
Declaration of Independence was the climax of a political
revolution which began in a spiritual emancipation. Our
delectable freedom came out of a vast and noble courage; it
is the direct result of a lofty and invincible religious spirit.

Suppose we go back and take a good long look at what really happened.

American colonial oppression started when Mother England passed and attempted to enforce the despicable Navigation Acts of 1651 and 1660, which restricted American shipping and exporting, and demanded that American products be sold only to the British Isles or to British possessions. That was the first spark to the Revolutionary kindling. One hundred years later, at the tender age of twenty-one, George III—dull, uneducated, bigoted and neurotic to the point of insanity—came to the throne. He acted immediately on the premise that a colony existed for one purpose and one purpose only: to enrich the mother country. Oppression followed oppression. Insult was heaped upon insult, until the patience of the colonists was exhausted, and the smoldering volcano let go. Patrick Henry put their case and their desperation into one volcanic question: "Is life so dear, or peace so sweet, as to be purchased at the price of chains and slavery?"

It followed as the night the day that *all* the colonies should cry "Amen!" to Henry's statement, and, later, to the Declaration of Independence, the explosive signal of a universal discontent which was to bring light and life to the New World.

A Continental Congress was called in 1774 to meet in Philadelphia, "to consult on the present state of the colonies; and to deliberate on wise and proper measures for the recovery of their just rights and liberties; and the restoration of union and harmony between Great Britain

and the Colonies, most ardently desired by all good men."
The Colonists proposed to stand upon their rights as
Englishmen. They forwarded a petition to the King, which
he refused to receive.

The Second Continental Congress was called in May,
1775, within a month after the battles of Lexington and
Concord. The war was now on; the Americans had begun
to defend what they believed to be "their ancient rights,"
but they soon discovered that there were new rights to be
acquired as well as old ones to be defended. When they
drew up their immortal Declaration they crystallized the
sentiments not only of oppression-weary America, but of a
chain-bound humanity everywhere.

On June 11, 1776, a committee was appointed to prepare
the Declaration; included on this committee were John
Adams, Benjamin Franklin, and Thomas Jefferson. After
full discussion in several meetings, the committee designated the thirty-three-year-old Virginian, Thomas Jefferson, to prepare the first draft of the Declaration because
he had, as John Adams put it, "a reputation of literature,
science, and a happy talent of composition."

Jefferson was a Virginian, a philosopher, a farmer, an
architect, an inventor (he designed the first revolving
chair and the first dumb-waiter), a talented lawyer, and a
good horseman. He had assembled a notable library of
books which he not only possessed, but read; he was well
acquainted with music and familiar with all the arts. He
was a voluminous writer, maintaining a prodigious correspondence. He had been governor of his native state during

63

the most anxious period of the Revolutionary War. He was the author of the Virginia Statute of Religious Liberty, separating Church from State, an act passed by the legislature seven years after its initiation and when Jefferson was no longer a member of the body. He compiled a Bible of his own, which, by resolution of the Fifty-seventh Congress was printed in an edition of 9,000 copies and was known as *The Jefferson Bible*. He was not skillful as a politician, nor was he particularly eloquent as a speaker, but he had an eager and a daring mind. His knowledge was as catholic as his gifts were versatile, and as father of the University of Virginia he inspired a love of knowledge and truth in all who came after him.

This was the man who was the chief ideological exponent of the American Revolution—a citizen of considerable wealth and of high social position, an aristocrat among aristocrats, and still a democrat among democrats.

Jefferson sat in the parlor of his second-floor lodging at the corner of Seventh and Market Streets in Philadelphia and, without consulting a single book or pamphlet, wrote in a half-day's time our great national confession of faith, the rough draft of which may now be seen in the Library of Congress. He submitted it first to John Adams, who made two corrections, and then to Benjamin Franklin, who made five other minor revisions. Thereafter it was submitted to the entire committee and approved without change. Jefferson's document was presented to Congress on June 28, 1776, and was laid on the table until July 1. On the second of July the resolution of acceptance was acted

64

on, but it was not until July 4 that the Declaration of Independence was adopted and proclaimed.

Unlike some of the frustrated and discontented liberals of our day who are often easy prey for the subtle and subversive forces of revolution, these liberal revolutionaries of 1776 were men of solid substance, representing every stratum of society. They were men of strength, native intelligence, and indomitable character. They were neither old men in their dotage nor foolhardy youths. Samuel Adams was fifty-three; John Hancock, thirty-nine; R. H. Lee, forty-four; Benjamin Harrison, thirty-six; John Adams, forty; Thomas Jefferson, thirty-three; Benjamin Franklin, seventy; Roger Sherman, fifty-five; and R. R. Livingston, twenty-nine.

The President of the College of New Jersey, the Reverend John Witherspoon, was the only clergyman to sign the Declaration. He is too much forgotten in our history books; John Witherspoon had a far-reaching influence on our democracy. He had taught several of the signers of the document, and nine of them were graduates of the little college over which he presided at Princeton. When he took up his pen to put his name to this document, Witherspoon declared:

There is a tide in the affairs of men, a nick of time. We perceive it now before us. To hesitate is to consent to our own slavery. That noble instrument upon your table, that insures immortality to its author, should be subscribed this very morning by every pen in this house. He that will not respond to its accents, and strain every nerve to carry into effect its provisions,

65

is unworthy of the name of free man. . . . For my own part, of property, I have some; of reputation, more. That reputation is staked, that property is pledged on the issue of this contest; and although these grey hairs must soon descend into the sepulcher, I would infinitely rather that they descend thither by the hand of the executioner than desert at this crisis the sacred cause of my country.

It is almost impossible for us to realize the dangers our forefathers were inviting when they signed this audacious instrument. It must have been in God's providence that the appointed time had come for the creation of this Declaration, for its adoption had an instant and epochal effect. It enkindled joy and quickened zeal for freedom. It separated patriots from loyalists. It encouraged people to endure hardships and privation for the cause of freedom. It prompted the Continental soldier to plunge into the fight with a new and dauntless courage and determination. It changed a war started on the defensive for the redress of wrongs into a war for the establishment of a free and separate government. From that Fourth of July to this present hour, it has been the inspiration for the oppressed of every people and nation in this earth.

This event, and what followed it, was primarily a spiritual movement. We cannot understand America unless we first understand that. Men's minds and souls were to be free—free to build a new world. The new world was to have a new faith, a faith that would spread everywhere. "God, who gave us life, gave us liberty," wrote Jefferson. The new nation was God-originated and God-destined.

66

The Declaration of Independence was a proclamation of universal human rights, and the world has not yet caught up with it.

we declare these truths to be self-evident, that all men are created equal; that they are endowed by their Creator with certain inalienable rights; that among these are life, liberty, and the pursuit of happiness.

Liberty and equality were not something achieved by men, but bestowed by God in His creative wisdom. Doubtless Jefferson knew that as a matter of present fact all men were not yet equal in endowment in their liberties and in their rights. But he knew that they ought to be and that one day they would be, and he declared it to be his faith and the faith of the new nation that all men, thus deriving their dignity and value from the Creator, must in the end be free men.

There were, of course, a few who signed the Document who believed it a good wartime creed, but not likely to be very successful on a permanent basis. Jefferson himself was not so sure that the Revolution would succeed by its first impact, but he believed that it was bound to succeed in the end.

Some critics suggest that Jefferson was too optimistic about human nature, that he was naïve and superficial in his doctrine of man. They are wrong. Jefferson knew the weaknesses of human nature, for he himself was at times the victim of vilification and the object of men's baser manifestations. He made bold to say, "I have sworn upon

67

the altar of God eternal hostility against any form of tyranny over the mind of man." He was aware that only free minds could make a free world, and that the only real freedom man possesses is that which he gains, not by personal attainment, but within his nature as the gift of his Creator.

The Declaration of Independence, in which this man has expressed for all time our American faith, marked one of the great periods in the progressive emancipation of the mind and spirit.

Before the sixteenth century attempts had been made to reform both the Church and medieval life. But, despite the influences of St. Francis and St. Dominic and many other good and noble men, rebirth was stifled until the ground swell of discontent and the passion for purity burst forth in the Reformation. Wherever this Reformation faith and Gospel have gone, life has been changed, men have recovered a sense of their own dignity, freedom has flourished, education has advanced, and society has been improved.

Although many streams came together at the confluence of time on July 4, 1776, the most significant of all was the stream of light generated by this Protestant Reformation. Faith in God, in the most real sense, was the heritage of our founding fathers. Apart from faith in God, our origin and our history have no meaning. From the beginning until yesterday's prayer in Congress our national life has been undergirded by this faith. In it our noblest institutions have been created, our culture promoted, our philan-

68

thropic endeavors initiated, our liberties secured, and freedom fostered for men everywhere. Men accustomed to freedom in their personal approach to God insisted on freedom in the public expression of their ideas and the ordering of their lives. It follows inevitably that when you strike the shackles from the soul you strike them from the mind and heart and wrists as well.

Jefferson was not an evangelical Christian; he was a deist. But he could state for the men of his day, nurtured as they were in the spirit of freedom, what they believed basically about God and human dignity. Men could be trusted with their own and other men's destinies and be truly free men only so long as they lived in obedience to a higher authority—the authority of God. Men who are obedient to God and who are submissive to his sovereign will are less in need of the laws of man and yet are most likely to be obedient to whatever laws are needed. The soul of man can be free only when it is captive to God.

So we cannot understand American history except as a spiritual movement. The eternal God is the source of its creation, and His Spirit the guide of its development. The American people covenanted with God, not as a local, continental, or racial deity, but as the living, universal God who, while being the God of all people, becomes in a special sense the God of all those who accept His purpose and do His will in human life.

Our nationhood began, continues, and ends in God. "In the name of God. Amen." was written above the first governmental document drawn up in the Mayflower Cabin.

69

"In God We Trust," confronts us on our humblest coins. Whether we think of the British Puritan in New England, of the Anglican in Virginia, of the Irish and Scotch and Germans in Pennsylvania, of the Dutch or of the Scandinavians, sterling Christian faith is common to them all.

Reflect, if you will, on colonial life, where at the center of each community there was a minister of religion known as "The Parson"—a term derived from an Anglo-Saxon word meaning "The Person." The parson in the Colonies was quite a person—he was the chief citizen in the community, in culture, and in learning. In these days, when the pew is often wiser than the pulpit, it is well to remember that the democratic life with its broad privileges of education, library, art, and music, came largely from what the Parson and his Church represented.

Several other forces at work in history had their influence on the newly emerging life when American freedom was born; there was, for instance, the Renaissance, the rise of humanism and the Industrial Revolution—but the Protestant Christian faith was the strongest determinative influence. Of the more than three million people in the thirteen colonies at the time of the Declaration of Independence, only twenty-two thousand were non-Protestant Christians. These people insisted on the immediacy of man's relation to God. To them, man's reconciliation with God was not something initiated by man but offered freely and joyously from the hand of God. For them the Bible was the norm of spiritual authority, the infallible rule of faith and life. For them, each man had the right to come directly before God; he was his own avenue of approach. Inevitably, there followed from this faith the exercise of private judgment and the principle of individual responsibility.

Wherever such men went they stressed the importance of religious freedom. They resisted coercion by either political or ecclesiastical authorities. The churches were then (and they continue to be) the real schools of democracy. This was the faith which had the great decisive influence on the new world.

One of the great scholars of Harvard, Samuel E. Morrison, inquiring into our origins, concludes:

No one who has delved deeply into the origin and history of the Colonies can by any fair application of the rules of evidence deny that the dynamic force in settling New England was English Puritanism desiring to realize itself. The leaders whom the people followed proposed, like Milton, to make over a portion of the earth in the spirit of Christian philosophy: a new church and state, family and school, ethic and conduct. They might and did differ among themselves as to the realization of these high and holy aims, but a city of God was their aim. Religion should permeate every phase of living. Man belongs to God alone; his only purpose in life is to enhance God's glory and to do His will; and every variety of human activity, every sort of human activity, every sort of human conduct presumably unpleasing to God must be discouraged if not suppressed.

This spirit, mediated to the life of America by a variety of denominations, promoted a sense of religious vocation in civic and business life. All work was made honorable

71

and all men were honored. The individual became of prime importance. Private initiative was encouraged. By and by, as the products of toil and business enterprise accumulated, they were less and less often hoarded or used selfishly; to an extent unparalleled in all previous history they were devoted to great causes—civic, cultural, philanthropic, and missionary. Christian missionaries were the first American internationalists, and they were this country's greatest ambassadors of good will to all parts of the globe.

The vast enterprise that is America was derived from a sense of spiritual origin and spiritual destiny—a sense of mission, derived from faith in a Sovereign God.

Political democracy, as we know it, is directly derived from our religious principles; and our instruments of government, in many of their aspects, can find their antecedent expressions in our free church government. Men of the Reformed tradition, nurtured in the spirit of freedom, believed that men who had faith in God and in human dignity could and would make a worthy nation.

Let me repeat it: *there is only one kind of true freedom, and that is freedom under God.* Without God, man is in unhappy rebellion and anarchy. When men do not fear God, they follow their own willfulness; in the end they become captive to their own sins, slaves to evil, destitute of inner illumination and cut off from the source and center of power. Such men cannot be trusted with their own destiny.

Lacking faith in God, men become lawless, and break

out in epidemics of crime; men without faith require maximum external power and force to control them and to destroy the evil which they represent. The New Testament is filled with these convictions. For, as we shall note in a later chapter, when men do not have this faith they become their own law. The immovable truth of history is that men under God possess a higher sense of moral responsibility and ethical discrimination. It is truth that "where the spirit of the Lord is, there is liberty."

Guizot once asked James Russell Lowell, "How long do you think the American Republic will endure?" And Lowell replied, "So long as the ideas of its founding fathers continue to be dominant."

Democracy, as we know it, depends on religion—the Christian religion. If our democracy should vanish, it would be because we have not been sufficiently Christian. Our noblest ideas are religious ideas; our highest standards are religious standards; our most desired goals are religious goals. Allow religion to languish, and democracy begins to disintegrate. We cannot neglect religion or trifle with this inheritance and keep it. We deserve it only as we cherish and cultivate it. If we are faithful to our trust, then the greatest days of the United States are ahead.

A long time ago the Apostle Paul wrote, "Ye have been called unto liberty . . ." (Galatians 5:13), to a people with a trait not too uncommon among Christians of our own times. Like many of us, the Galatians were moved easily to fervent enthusiasms from which they too promptly recovered. It was to this characteristic that Paul addressed

73

himself. He was appalled that, having experienced the glorious redemptive freedom of the Gospel, they should so readily have turned back to the fetters of their former faith, with its binding legalism. Paul was entreating them to return to the life to which they had been drawn by the Gospel.

So today I entreat my fellow Americans: "Brethren, ye are called unto liberty. . . . Stand fast therefore in the liberty wherein Christ has made us free . . ." (Galatians 5:13). For liberty is the great American vocation:

> For He that worketh high and wise . . .
> Nor pauseth in His plan,
> Will tear the sun out of the skies
> Ere freedom out of man . . .
> For what avails the plow or sail
> Or land, or life, if freedom fail?
> *Ralph Waldo Emerson*

74

CHAPTER IV

The Sickle or the Cross?

Never shall I forget the capture of Lansberg Concentration Camp early one morning in the spring of 1945.

With the unexpectedly swift approach of our armored troops, the German camp authorities had been caught unprepared for our arrival. They had succeeded in moving a few of their wretched prisoners out of the compound; others had been moved as far as the railroad siding, where they had been slaughtered and their bodies—still warm and bleeding—littered the ground beside the train which they had never been permitted to board. Still others, locked in their huts, had been set afire. We saw their charred bodies among the smoldering ruins; contorted limbs and faces were grim evidence of their struggle to survive. Not a prisoner remained alive to enjoy the liberation which American troops would have brought them.

A few days earlier I had entered Dachau Concentration Camp. Nothing that has been written or photographed has adequately portrayed to the world what our young American troops discovered there. I had seen men killed on the battlefield, and I had been with them elsewhere when their lives came to an end, but this was the first time I had ever interviewed a man only to watch him walk a few yards away and drop dead of hunger and disease. Even those who were supposedly well and healthy in that camp were a sorry spectacle; the near-dead were a tragedy. But those already dead, heaped high like cordwood in and around a crematory, published the bestiality of the whole Nazi ideology and process.

Hosts of clergymen were among the political prisoners confined at Dachau; in a period of some five years 2,448 clergymen of varying faiths had been torn from their families, separated from their parishes and friends and imprisoned here because they obstructed the political "purity" and the military aims of the Third Reich. More than one thousand of the imprisoned clergy had died of disease or been deliberately murdered. Until the capture of the camp by the invading army only eight clergymen had been restored alive to their former homes.

In Hitler's Germany it was inevitable that religious leaders would be special targets for the wrath of the Nazi. In a State where the "chosen people" were pure Nordic history's ancient "chosen people," the Jews, could not exist.

76

In a State which deified its own reality and demanded absolute obedience of its citizens, an international ecclesiastical organism which in matters of faith demanded of its subjects allegiance to a foreign spiritual ruler could not be allowed to flourish, and thus the Roman Catholic could not be tolerated. In a State where the mind is enslaved and can entertain only ideas approved by the Party's leader, the Protestant with his free mind and direct access to God and outspoken convictions had to be silenced. So, for religious fidelity which produced political deviation, men of moral stamina and sensitive conscience suffered a violence which civilized man would shun even for the most desperate of criminals.

Having viewed these unspeakable demonstrations of man's inhumanity to man which were Dachau and Lansberg, I tried to analyze my feelings. In common with other Americans, my first reaction was one of intense indignation, especially as I reflected that these ghastly sights were multiplied many times over throughout Nazi Germany. Any man with decent moral standards could view such evidences of bestiality with nothing but profound disgust and revulsion.

My second reaction was that of pity and compassion for the physical suffering and mental anguish of the victims, and a deep admiration for the brave spirits whose only guilt lay in the fact that they had declined to co-operate with the Nazis or were disqualified from their rights of citizenship and property because of their race and faith.

77

But as the shock receded and my rational processes returned, I realized that I was an American and a Christian; standing there amid this devastation of the human spirit and the human body, there came over me a quiet feeling of thanksgiving that this could not possibly happen in my country. It was not a feeling of pride or self-righteousness, but a genuine gratitude that I was a citizen of a nation which still possessed a large measure of moral sensitivity and ethical discrimination. I could not conceive of this ever happening in America.

And yet how did it happen that Germany so long exposed to the same Christian faith as ours could thus degenerate? How could people of rich culture and refined spirit, exposed for many centuries to Christian influences, descend to such baseness? Is it enough to say that all this suffering was inflicted by a few hardened, neurotic men temporarily enslaved by the state? Or had something happened to the faith that was basic to the life of the nation? How was it that this people in central Europe, with a culture older than ours, could give way to this neo-paganism and synthetic barbarism?

For this was a synthetic barbarism—not primitive and tribal, but rather a barbarism superimposed on a once intelligent people, a barbarism armed with modern engines of destruction and diabolical devices of torture and motivated by dark, furtive forces.

I remembered being in Europe not very many years before the war began and hearing a group of fine-looking

78

young German lads swear allegiance to a Youths' National Socialist Creed which said something like this:

1. I believe that National Socialism is the only saving faith for Germany.
2. I believe in a God who has sent us Adolph Hitler.
3. I believe in a God who has sent us Adolph Hitler to to save us from becoming parasites and do-nothings.
4. I believe in a God who has sent us Adolph Hitler to bring us beauty and truth.

Millions of young Germans said, "I believe," to that sort of gruesome nonsense!

Here was a paganism as blatant and blasphemous as has appeared in more than two thousand years, with its worship of a man-God instead of the God-man, imputing to him the Messianic qualities of a saviour, and demanding for him and his state absolute commitment of body and soul. It was because the young German said, "I believe" this paganism, that he went out not only as a trained soldier armed with modern weapons, but as a flaming religious zealot armed with a philosophy born in hell.

Despite the influence of Christianity in Germany, a dark and demonic force had laid hold on her. Many said political and economic factors may have worked together to produce Hitler after World War I; but, whatever the factors, by the time World War II burst on mankind, it was an evil and deadly ideology with which we had to deal. The faith which motivated the Nazi was in direct conflict with the faith of the Christian. Long before our armies were fighting

79

the massive manifestation of this evil on the battlefield robust Christian souls were fighting it on the battlefields of the spirit; the world must ever be in debt to the brave men who stood up to the dark oppressors of the Nazi era and paid with their lives for their faith.

It is clear from this experience that Christian tradition alone, or the mere existence of a church, cannot save a people from paganism. Only Christian men committed to the utmost and a virile church bearing uncompromising witness can stand up against dynamic paganism.

This Nazi paganism was hardly subdued when another appeared on the horizon of free men. Today we are confronted with a new "world religion of salvation."

Make no mistake about it! Communism is more than economics, more than sociology, more than Russian nationalism on the warpath. Although rejecting God in the historic sense of that term, it evokes the total loyalty of its adherents to forces beyond the individual which are believed to be purposefully and inexorably at work in the universe. It is fanatically evangelistic in its quest for converts and it crusades by fair means and foul to extend the borders of its domain.

The personal pilgrimage of the new religion's founder is enlightening. Karl Marx, who fashioned its ideology, was first a Jew, then a Lutheran, and finally an atheist. He absorbed his concept of social justice from the Hebrew prophets, extending the idea to a belief that violent social change is inevitable. He acquired from Christianity the conception of a Day of Judgment, when the sins of society are condemned and made public and when heaven on earth is to become the reward of the oppressed of the world. He drew from atheism his belief that man and man alone would bring about the great Day of Judgment—through the revolution of the proletariat—and that on the final day the judgment throne would be occupied by man rather than by God.

To the three great religions of the world of Semitic origin—Christianity, Judaism, and Islam—we must now add a fourth: Communism. Only in the context of a world religion, competing for men's allegiance, can the issues of this epoch be understood. Communism makes its appeal as salvation, as a saving faith. The salvation which it offers is not "pie in the sky by and by," but salvation in the world here and now.

The religious competition of the age is pointed out by Dr. Charles Lowry in his analogy between Christianity and Communism. In his scholarly book, *Communism and Christ* (Copyright 1952-1953 by Morehouse-Gorham Co.), we find the following outline of the cardinal features of Communism as they might be interpreted in Christian terminology:

1. There is one living Creator, God, which is matter in motion, dialectically directed.
2. The Trinity—thesis, antithesis, and synthesis.
3. Three persons of revelation and worship—Marx, the law-giver, Lenin, the incarnate truth, and the Dictator, who is guide and comforter.

4. The Chosen People—the Proletariat, destined to inherit the earth.

5. Evil, which is sin and death—private property, the source of all social ills.

6. Redemption is by atonement—the blood of the proletariat.

7. The Church, the organ of truth and mediator of redemption—the Party, organ of action, enlightenment and discipline.

8. The Sacred Writings—those of Marx and Lenin, and the record of their deeds.

9. The law of the Kingdom of Heaven is the law of the classless society.

10. The Last Judgment, with its separation of the sheep and goats, saints and sinners, is to be found in Communism's violent overthrow of Capitalism and the enthronement of the Proletariat.

11. The Millennium will be the establishment of a universal, classless brotherhood.

12. To inspire all in this religion of salvation is the Real Presence—the ceaseless exposure of the perpetually renewed body of Lenin within the "holy sanctuary" of the Red Square.

Lowry has rendered a great service to the Church in his treatise, which is the best yet to come to my attention. A thorough study of his book would be profitable to those who want to obtain a deeper understanding of the ideological crisis of our times.

There are spiritual values at stake in the world crisis today which strike at the very roots of our very existence. The time has come for us to know exactly what it is we believe, why we believe it, and why we must resist that which would destroy us and destroy as well the faith that has made us what we are. Our faith and the way of life produced by our faith are in mortal peril. The Apostle Paul wrote to the Corinthian Christians in his day, "There be gods many and lords many" (Corinthians 8:5). So it is now with us.

Some in our time have become accustomed to thinking of Communism as a Christian heresy, and that somehow or other this heresy might become orthodox. It is a sad error. Communism stands in juxtaposition to our faith. The interesting parallel of features outlined above should make this clear. Communism is not an adaptation of Christianity, but a substitute for it. It is not a Christian heresy but a new world religion contending with Christianity for men's allegiance.

The philosophies now set in opposition to each other are irreconcilable. We might as well face the fact that should Communism engulf the world the Christian witness could survive only through suffering and martyrdom.

Some others have equated social amelioration with the Christian concept of the Kingdom of God. Perhaps this is where many American liberals got off the track in the twenties and thirties, and perhaps why some have not yet gotten back. Social service centers, workers' clubs, nurseries for working mothers, and medical services provided by the government may be helpful to the oppressed masses, but their existence does not mean that the Kingdom of God has arrived. To presume that the fulfillment of sociological blueprints and industrial and economic reforms are the achievement of the Kingdom of God is to get the sequence

83

wrong. It is a mistaken application of the Sermon on the Mount.

How was it that Jesus Christ came to change the world? He came to put God in the center of men's lives. "Jesus came into Galilee preaching the gospel of the kingdom of God, and saying, The time is fulfilled, and the kingdom of God is at hand: repent ye, and believe the gospel" (Mark 1:14, 15).

At the very opening of His ministry He went into the synagogue in Nazareth and taking up the Scriptures read from the prophecy of Isaiah, "The spirit of the Lord is upon me, because he hath anointed me to preach the gospel to the poor; he has sent me to heal the broken-hearted, to preach deliverance to the captives, and recovering of sight to the blind, to set at Liberty them that are bruised, to preach the acceptable year of the Lord" (Luke 4:18, 19). And then He announced, "This day the scripture is fulfilled in your ears." The Kingdom of God had come in Him; He was the Kingdom in miniature. The Man and the message were one. The program and the Person were inseparable. The rule of God in the hearts of men—that was the Kingdom He was proclaiming.

Everywhere He went He revealed God and interpreted God to men. Everywhere He went He urged men to repent of their sins and their wickedness and their folly and to put God at the center of their lives. It was seeing God and knowing God and having fellowship with God that was the burden of His appeal.

He bore witness of this truth in His life. As a boy, He

84

said, "Wist ye not that I must be about my Father's business?" When His disciples feared He might be hungry, He exclaimed, "I have meat to eat that ye know not of, for my meat is to do the will of him that sent me." In the garden of decision, He called out in anguish of spirit, "Not my will, but thine be done." At last, when His work was done and He went to His Cross, He exclaimed, "Father, into thy hands I commend my spirit." Everything He was, and everything He did, was to reveal the perfect God-centered, God-conscious life.

He came, not with a set of sociological blueprints or political theories or an economic program—though He did have a message for the sociologists, politicians, and economists. He offered no human Utopia. He was not a Titan who did many things well. He did one central thing perfectly. He revealed the life of God in the life of man. Men pleaded with Jesus to lead a revolution, to destroy tyranny, to command an army, to sit on a royal throne; He was urged to demonstrate His physical power—to turn stones into bread, to throw Himself down from the temple, to use His supernatural powers to achieve a wordly Kingdom. He kept on quietly talking about the Kingdom of God and demonstrating it in Himself. Into that world of human slavery, political intrigue and rigid class consciousness He came preaching and demonstrating the Gospel of the Kingdom of God. That was His message. The Kingdom and the King were one and inseparable.

Then He sent out His disciples. They proclaimed the Gospel that God in Christ had done a mighty work. The

King had come. They knew that His Kingdom was to come in the hearts of men, for it already had come in them. They asserted that the Kingdom of God could not come elsewhere until it was first established in men's hearts. They said that wicked men had rejected this King, had tried to dethrone Him, and finally attempted to destroy Him—but He lived; that He now called men to follow Him, to obey Him. In the name of this King they called for repentance and entrance into the Kingdom—the Kingdom in which God rules in the hearts of men.

That Gospel spread through the ancient world. That Gospel brought an upheaval in the social, economic, and political life of a world that was falling to pieces. But that Gospel was not merely a social, economic, or political program. It was a Gospel which began by first changing men's personalities, giving them a new focal center and a new point of reference. Men who were themselves changed began changing their institutions.

When men are born into the Kingdom of God and experience the love of God something happens. How different from the bitter hate and ruthless cruelty of the Communist! Men in the Kingdom of God can be slaves neither to men nor to institutions. That is why freedom was born in the Gospel. When we "put God at the center of life" men can be trusted. When a world makes the God of our Lord Jesus Christ paramount, then the world can be trusted. It was to redeem men for the Kingdom of God that Jesus came into the world.

86

Many within the Church have misunderstood the meaning of the Kingdom. They have the sequence wrong. They have tried to bring in the Kingdom without the King. They have too readily equated social progress, political platforms and economic reforms with the Kingdom of God, without God's spirit in the hearts of men and at the center of their programs. They have insisted that this must be done because it is based on the Sermon on the Mount. They have forgotten that the famous sermon was not uttered to a miscellaneous throng of unconverted men, but rather to disciples who were already committed to the King; that sermon was presented to the little band that had withdrawn from the multitudes to a mountain retreat. "And seeing the multitudes, he went up into a mountain and when he was set, his disciples came unto him. And he opened his mouth and taught them, saying . . ." (Matt. 5:1, 2).

The words were spoken to men who recognized and accepted the King and were ready to live in the Kingdom of God. They were not spoken to unredeemed, uncommitted men. It is one thing to apply the Beatitudes to the people for whom they were intended; it is quite another thing to assume that these standards are completely applicable to a spiritually miscellaneous or unconverted people. The standards of the Kingdom belong to those who acknowledge the King and live in the Kingdom.

It is because we have often attempted the establishment of the Kingdom without the King that the Church shares with the rest of mankind the guilt for the present tragic hour. Too many have thought that the Kingdom of God

87

is simply a world without war, in which there are better houses, better pay, and more leisure. Some churchmen have said, "If only we can have a world in which peace prevails, in which there is no coercion, and where men are well fed, well housed, and well clothed, then we will have the Kingdom of God." Would we have the Kingdom even if there were no coercion, no war, and universal peace? Do you have the Kingdom when truth is suppressed? Do you have the Kingdom when personality is defamed? Do you have the Kingdom when there is slavery? Do you have the Kingdom when fellowship is obstructed by the imprisonment of multitudes behind an Iron Curtain?

The Church has been right in promoting world peace. Certain sections of the Church have been wrong in supposing that pacifism as a national policy could be effective in the presence of today's evils.

The Church has been right in insisting that international conflicts be resolved by peaceful adjudication through the United Nations. It has been wrong when it supposed that in the present world such efforts could be successful without the adequate implementation of military force, for it is clear now that the world crisis, while being a clash of ideologies and political theories, is also a collision of powers. To be weak and irresolute is to invite failure. We are in danger of being unable to deal with realities, including moral realities. The United Nations, United States, and the whole free world are threatened by men who have acquired tremendous military power at the moment; they seem to understand only the language of such power.

The Church has been right in insisting that we share food, clothing, medicines, tools and technical skills with the dispossessed and underprivileged of the world, the absence of which gives Communism its chance to move in. It has been wrong, as all men are wrong, in supposing that these material satisfactions alone would bring in the Kingdom of God.

It is equally wrong to suppose that military power *alone* will solve the whole question. All we have been saying points up the urgency of the crisis for evangelical Christianity. Some of us have been entertaining hopes that the leaders of Communism could be converted—or radically modified—and the world thereby reconciled. It is our Christian vocation to work for and believe in the conversion of all men to God through Jesus Christ. We must never forsake that divine commission which Christ Himself has given us. Indeed, conversion of the leaders who threaten the peace and well-being of the world is perhaps our best hope of averting disaster. We should be encouraged by the fact that Communists *have* been converted to Christ and His Church. One of the major competitions with which Communism confronts the Church is its quest for conversion. If men without deep religious faith sometimes are converted to Communism, which is atheistic, how much more readily should we expect the conversions of Communists to Christianity, with all the resources of God available to Christ's emissaries? We must reckon with the present inaccessibility of the Communist leaders and

89

the present limitations on the work and spread of Christian missions. But we need not stop praying and working. Prayer has penetrated barriers which politics could never surmount.

Let us then as evangelical Christians clearly understand the spiritual nature of the present crisis. Volumes have been written and can yet be written, discussing the complicated forces and cross currents of movements and mixed philosophies which are part of our present world order.

The spiritual significance of the world crisis may not be easy to determine and analyze, nor as simple as black and white, but neither is it so complex as is sometimes supposed. And it is not so difficult that the zealous, prayerful evangelical Christian cannot understand it and, understanding it, contend for the faith that was once and for all time delivered unto him.

When you read the history of our country in the light of the New Testament, you can come to no conclusion other than that our kind of democracy has been created and sustained by Christian conviction and faith. In I Corinthians 7:22, we read, "For he that is called in the Lord, being a servant, is the Lord's freeman: likewise, also he that is called, being free, is Christ's servant." The Christian is a free man only because he is a servant. He is liberated because he is committed in a higher loyalty to God. He is not free to do as he pleases; he is free only to glorify God. His freedom is under God's sovereignty. He is a free man because he has become captive to Christ. The familiar hymn puts it, "Make me a captive, Lord, and then I shall be free."

Men who are redeemed and restored to their pristine state and who live and move and have their being in God can be trusted. They can be trusted because their loyalty is to, and their direction derived from, a higher power. Men free under God can be trusted because they voluntarily accept spiritual disciplines; they are amenable to the guidance of God and obedient to His will. This truth is the crux of the matter: our way of life can be had and can be preserved only so long as there exists a dedicated and disciplined corps of Christians who know that all we are and all we have is under God.

Understanding the differences between Christianity and Communism is not merely an academic exercise. It sharpens our own faith and gives purpose to our living.

The Christian begins by faith in God—God as a living reality, God as a personal being, God as sovereign ruler of the universe, who holds all creation in his hands, to whom supreme allegiance is given, and to whom the immortal souls of men are accountable. Communism rejects the reality of God and substitutes an atheistic and materialistic absolutism. Ultimate reality, Communism asserts, lies in matter and matter alone. It capitalizes on the religious spirit in man, but teaches that there is no God above the Party and therefore makes absolute a human and finite reality. In rejecting God and His righteousness Communism fails also to understand sin and wickedness—the corrupting effect of pride, self-centeredness, and the will to power.

Christianity proclaims the dignity and worth of individual man. The first thing we say about human nature is that man is created in the image of God, and that although he has fallen from his first state and become a sinner, he may be restored to the dignity of his created state. The only reason man merits respect and honor is that he is the created son of God. The freedom and the dignity which man has is his, not as a personal achievement, but as something he possesses as a gift of God through creation.

This conception gives Christians a different attitude toward their fellow beings. The only reason for treating other persons with respect at all is that they are God's creatures endowed with an eternal destiny. You cannot treat a man as a piece of machinery if you believe him to be a living soul and the creation of God. Communism rejects this conception of man and thereby devalues man. Man has value, according to Communism, only in relation to and in the service of the collective society. The chief end of man, therefore, is not to glorify God, but to serve the collective entity—be it of party or of state. That is why the Communists have no disturbed conscience in resorting to unbridled police methods, liquidations, concentration camps, and all the other violations of human dignity which are a part of the Communist pattern.

At no other point is the difference so great as in these views of man. Devaluating man, there develops within Communism an intense class consciousness. "The dictatorship of the proletariat" is in itself an assertion of class consciousness. All other classes are denounced and liquidated; only those approved by the Party are tolerated.

Soviet Russia, where this experiment has been tried longest, is the most class-conscious area of the world. Communist propaganda talks about "the people," but "the people" of that part of the world are not "the people" as we understand them in America. The only people who count in Russia are those who favor the Communist regime. All opponents. whom *we* would call "people," are soon labeled as anti-democratic forces, or as enemies of the people, and thus do not count at all. Over and over again, we have discovered this principle in the satellite countries. It is this devaluation of man as a person that leads to tyranny.

Paul Robeson laments our cruel and un-Christian race discrimination in America and exalts the Soviet order into a fantastic heaven which it cannot possibly be. Let us grant that we must make our race relations more Christian, but let Mr. Robeson understand that he has lost all sense of perspective and human values. In America we are at least striving to make our way more Christian and to put justice and charity into our treatment of all groups, especially minority groups. Let Mr. Robeson and all others of his mind recognize that there is nothing in American life which stresses difference of class and race as it is stressed in his Russian Utopia—where the bourgeois and the capitalist are hunted like animals, where persons deemed unorthodox are terrorized and liquidated, where multitudes are tracked down and placed in concentration camps

93

or slave-labor units, simply because they do not agree with the government.

While Communism professes a philosophy which says, "From each according to his ability, to each according to his need," there is nevertheless a great differentiation in the economic rewards which are meted out to certain notorious "comrades." During a visit to Russia in the mid-Thirties, I was somewhat startled to observe how large were the incomes of artists and writers in the propaganda industry and how lucrative were the rewards given plant managers and farm superintendents—and how pitifully small was the income of the luckless common man.

The Stakhanovite movement is really an appeal to the profit motive and a spur to individual wealth. Under it individuals are rewarded for successes in what we call "piece-time work"; they are honored with extra pay and with cultural and recreational privileges. Members of the Party, administrators, social engineers, factory and farm supervisors become increasingly rich in contrast with the average Russian.

In America, during the same period, because of our system of taxation and our generous response to benevolent enterprises, there has been a general lessening in the wealth retained by individuals with large incomes. Nevertheless, while the Russians have been experimenting, the living standard of the average American has phenomenally improved. This does not tell the whole story, but it does say something for our view of man and his destiny.

Christianity, with its faith in God and its belief in the

94

dignity of man, believes also in a fixed point of moral reference. Some things are eternally right and some things are eternally wrong. As one of the Justices of our Supreme Court put it long ago, "The Ten Commandments will not budge."

For Communists there is no transcendent judgment. In their view, when the rulers of a nation disown God, they become responsible to no one but themselves and recognize no morality and no conduct except that which achieves their own ends. Absolute authority in Communism is reposed in the leaders or in the Party. Anything is moral which achieves the Party's objectives, and that includes lies, deceit, barbarism, liquidation. In countries where Communism is in power lying, stealing, and killing do not have the same moral meaning that they have for us. This fact is due to differing views of the nature of man and his soul. And it is this fact which makes it difficult for us to come to any trustworthy agreement with the Communists; this is the stumbling-block that tries the patience of diplomats and makes peaceful negotiation so exasperating and unfruitful.

In his significant and timeless book, *Heritage and Destiny* (Macmillan), Dr. John Mackay points out that nations may be distinguished from one another by the attitudes which they take toward God and the divine. Three such attitudes, he says, are observable.

The first is the "secular" nation, which considers that public welfare demands the complete elimination of God from all official relations with its life and culture. Its supreme loyalty, it says, is not to God but to ideas. Its heritage is not deity but ideology. The second type is the "demoniac" nation. This describes a nation which has transformed itself into an ultimate which takes the place of God, or which has deified some reality associated with its life. It makes absolute something which is purely relative and finite. This is a characteristic of totalitarian nations.

The third is the "covenant" nation, which recognizes its dependence upon God and its responsibility towards God. This is the nation which acknowledges in its instruments of government and national institutions that God is the source and being of its life and culture. (Copyright 1943. Used by permission of the Macmillan Company.)

Ours has been a Covenant nation. Our forefathers covenanted with God in a unique sense and acknowledged that Covenant in the founding documents and in the institutions of our country. In the United States of America God is acknowledged as the source of human rights. Our governmental documents make it clear that it is not to reason or to revolution that we owe our liberty, but to the fact that God made man. Not natural resources, nor wealth, nor scientific advancement, nor rugged individualism is the essence of American life; rather it is that this people convenanted with God to be the servant of His purpose. God is recognized as the source of human rights. Therefore, the highest rôle this nation can play is to reflect God's righteousness in national policies and to promote His Glory in all its relationships.

It may be that the early Christians, who were a subjugated people living in an occupied province of a vast empire in whose government they did not participate, could be detached for a while from the concerns of their faith as it related to the world about them. In such circumstances they could even remain pacifist. Since they had no responsibility and did not share in the determination of the world's destiny, they did not bear the heavy obligations that devolve on Christians in the United States today. Because the source of our life is what it is, and because we are what we are, we must dedicate ourselves more resolutely to the faith we have inherited. The time is short for a rebirth of spirit which will undergird us for the intensified struggle. But the Spirit, working in us, may make us a greater force than we have ever dreamed we could be. It is the Spirit that will make the difference.

The Communists and their sympathizers may for a time outnumber Christians of the world, but if we have the faith we claim to have, and if we really believe and practice what we profess, we shall be indestructible.

The most important thing for us to do today is to set over against Communism a more vital and more Christian society. A tepid church and a half-hearted Christianity cannot possibly deal with the dynamism set against us.

The only way to fight a false religion is with a true religion, and a true religion cannot be a soft, easy-going, complacent, nominal, Sunday-go-to-meeting religion. It means a New Christianity—more real, more intense, and more vital than we have known before. It means not words, but deeds. It means not utterance, but faith radically applied.

97

The call is clear. It is to live by this faith in God, in man's dignity and in moral certitude. It is to be willing and ready to pay whatever price is necessary to make the way of God the way for the sons of God. Only by exalting Jesus Christ and really putting Him first in our lives shall we as a nation be able to maintain the cross above the sickle.

~~~~~~

CHAPTER V

Recovering Our Foundations

Both before and after the Revolution there was a great surging movement to conquer and push back the American frontier, develop the natural resources of the New World and establish a new nation; life became something more than mere physical survival and the selfish exploitation of a rich land. The American pioneer who planned this movement was a man of physical strength reinforced by superior intelligence, inspired by a worthy dream, and endowed with a spirit determined to bring that dream to reality.

He faced the forest and the future with three powerful weapons in his hands: he carried an axe, a gun, and a Book.

With the axe he attacked the forests, hewed logs for his house, his school, and his church. With the gun he hunted game for his table and animal pelts for a livelihood, and protected himself against the predatory forces of the wilderness. The Book was the center of his personal devotions, the inspiration of his institutions and the textbook of his education.

Gathered into a community, this hardy pioneer quickly placed two institutions at the base of his community living: he built early and well his church and his public school (strange, isn't it, that those two buildings are still the most important buildings in any American town?). And the leading citizen of the early American community, at least in piety and learning, was, as we have already said, the "parson"; no other personage in our history has so influenced the life of the average citizen as has this human phenomenon who was at once preacher, schoolmaster, interpreter of the passing scene, and advisor in all forms of endeavor.

These parsons represented a widely divided Protestantism—a situation often seized upon with great glee by our anti-church critics, but a situation not so bad, after all, when we see it in true perspective. We must remember that the divisions of early American Protestantism were just so much ecclesiastical confusion brought over here from Europe. From England came embattled Methodists, Congregationalists, Baptists, and Anglicans; from Scotland, Switzerland, and northern Ireland came the Presbyterians; from France, Holland, Switzerland, and the Netherlands came the Reformed groups; from Germany and Scandinavia, the Lutherans; and Roman Catholics, later in the day, poured in from southern Ireland, Spain, Portugal,

France, Italy and other southern European states. Into the American melting pot were poured the strengths and weaknesses of all these conflicting and confusing religious bodies of the Old World. We did not invent our denominational differences in Protestantism; we inherited them from Europe.

Divided they certainly were in the colonies—yet there was strength in their division. For division was the logical fruit of a common struggle for freedom. Their rebellion against the autocracy of the Old World churches had already begun when they stepped ashore in the New World; they were merely transferring the locale of the battle. They had insisted in Europe that every man should be free to seek and worship God in his own way, and for thinking that they were "harried out of the land." The protest ripened here into a revolt that was not only religious, but social, political and economic as well. Every man was a king in the early American church; every man was peculiarly the child of God, and as such entitled to his own unhampered quest for life, liberty, and happiness. Individualism, not conformity, was the order of the new day.

American democracy owes its greatest debt to the nonconformists of this divided Colonial church; in this dissenters' paradise rebellion in the church fostered rebellion in the states. The fierce struggle for religious liberty had more influence on our struggle for political liberty than most of us imagine.

After the struggle—tolerance! Our forefathers taught us how to live together in unity of spirit in the midst of religious diversity. They created a tolerance and a deep sense of religious freedom out of which came the American Way. It is impossible to account for modern America otherwise, just as it is impossible to think of a free state without first thinking of a free church.

Suppose we look, for a moment, at the influence of those early churches. There were, first of all, the transplanted Anglicans of old England. These were almost unanimously Loyalist and Tory—naturally, considering that their church in England had been the Church of England! They were more closely bound to the mother country than any other Colonial church—but let it be said quickly that these same "Anglicans" contributed the largest number of signers to the Declaration of Independence of any Church body in the Colonies, and that since 1776 they have given us Presidents and national leaders in numbers all out of proportion to their church membership. They have built a great Protestant Episcopal Church that is still one of the most important religious groups on American soil.

The Methodists, like the Anglicans, had close ties with England—so close that by 1779 nearly every British-bred, British-born and British-ordained Methodist preacher in the Colonies had fled either to Canada or home to England. American preachers took over, however, and when the surrender came at Yorktown the American Methodists had eighty preachers and fourteen thousand members. By the time of the Civil War Abraham Lincoln could "thank God for the Methodists, who have sent more prayers to heaven and more men to the front than any other church

102

in the land." With their evangelistic fervor and social passion, they have penetrated every area of American life, building churches and colleges and hospitals from coast to coast; they have built up the largest single Protestant membership (more than nine million) in the United States.

The Baptists appeared early in the colonies, and at several points. They faced struggle and persecution—out of which came Roger Williams (called "the Father of American religious liberty") and Rhode Island. An early Baptist historian said, "Our religious education agrees with, and perfectly corresponds with, a government by the people." Their peculiar form of church government emphasized the compact, the equality of all men before God and congregational autonomy; it held within itself the seeds of republicanism and democracy. In the northeast, middle, and southern colonies, the Baptists were the largest single church body committed to an irrepressible campaign for the separation of church and state.

The Congregationalists of New England—who can estimate their contribution? Their preachers sparked the American Revolution. Ridicule or condemn them as you will for their stiff-necked Puritanism, there was nevertheless a moral and spiritual strength and splendor in the Puritan which passed into the blood stream of our nation at just the right moment, and which contributed mightily to our success in the Revolution.

The Lutherans brought their Martin Luther: who ever brought a nobler spirit to these shores? They brought also a distrust of tyranny and war from Germany and the

Scandinavian peninsula. From Germany, too, came the pietist sects—Mennonites, Moravians, Schwenkfelders, Dunkers—with their firm allegiance to the basic doctrines of primitive Christianity, an unconquerable faith in the inner spirit of man, in individual judgment and freedom of conscience and informal worship and the sovereignty of the congregation and of every individual in the congregation. They stood apart from the struggles of colonial politics, but their courage and sincerity and simplicity were good solid bricks in the house of American liberty.

The Quakers held doctrines that were democratic to the core; they preached and practiced brotherhood and brotherly love, mutual dependence and assistance, abstinence from war, justice for all, the abolition of priestly authority, and an all-out religious individualism. They contributed the only real martyrs to religious persecution in the Colonies; in early Pennsylvania they showed the world what a free, Christian colony could be like—the most Christian and most American of all the colonies. The colonies where they had power were the most democratic colonies; their influence went deeper than most of us admit.

The Roman Catholics were not numerous at first; they were slow to come. Until after the Revolution, Roman Catholics in New York were obliged to go all the way to Philadelphia to attend mass! But at the call of developing American industry they began to arrive in larger and larger numbers. They poured into the larger cities, and in the cities today they still have their major strength. The

Roman Catholic Church is now the largest single church in America.

The Jewish faith flourished here as it has seldom flourished elsewhere. Although he represents only five per cent of the population, the Jew, with his belief in a common God and Father for all mankind, has vastly enriched our culture.

The eternal God has His own plan for mankind. The religious bodies of America, in strength and weakness, have been the conveyors of His Spirit, and by His providence and their help America has risen to her present stature among the nations of the earth.

Now, I happen to be a Presbyterian, and you will forgive me if as a Presbyterian—and a Calvinist—I am somewhat interested in the manner in which the followers of John Calvin have poured so many red corpuscles into the American blood stream. Suppose we look for a moment at some of their contributions, which have become warp and woof of our democratic structure.

Vast segments of the colonial population were Calvinistic in their theology and in their attitude toward life. "Cousin America," said Horace Walpole to a British Parliament, "has run off with a Presbyterian parson." Their allegiance to Presbyterianism, he thought, was at the heart of their rebellion. He may have been right at that. Four-fifths of the ministers in colonial America were tinctured by Calvinism, and more than half the men Washington commanded were either Presbyterian or otherwise influenced by the Calvinistic faith. In more than one Revolutionary battle entire

companies were made up of Presbyterian soldiers commanded by their pastors and officered by their elders. Who
can forget the parson at the Battle of Springfield who, when
paper for wadding in the Continental muskets ran short,
rushed into his little Presbyterian church near the battlefield and out again with his arms loaded down with hymn-
books which featured the hymns of Isaac Watts, shouting
to the Continentals, "Give 'em Watts, boys, give 'em
Watts!"

When Washington was asked one day if he would ever
surrender, he replied that he would not; if things were to
collapse, he would retreat into the mountains with an army
made up of Scotch-Irish Presbyterians and fight on forever!

At least two-thirds of the Colonists were instructed in
Calvinism, for about nine hundred thousand of the three-
million population were of Scotch or Scotch-Irish descent.
That numerical strength alone, if not the virility of their
faith, would account for the historian Ranke's statement
that "John Calvin is the practical founder of America."

Thus one did not have to be a prophet to determine just
where a Presbyterian would be found fighting in any battle
for freedom. For the Presbyterians had not forgotten their
long border feuds and the horrible struggles in the home-
land against the assaults and persecutions of British mon-
archs. You would never find a Calvinist fighting *for* a king.
Someone has described a Calvinist as a man who "bends
one knee before God and the other on the neck of a king."
It isn't a bad description.

But most of the Presbyterian contributions were far

more constructive than merely fighting on the right side in a war. They put great traditional emphasis on covenant and compact with God; they insisted on a well-educated ministry; they founded colleges in order to obtain such a ministry; Scotch to the core, they had more than their share of common sense in both philosophy and theology, and, notwithstanding their bitter background of persecution, they were more tolerant than most of their contemporary churches. On the whole, it might be safe to say that the Scotch-Irish were more tolerant and democratic in politics and in their social attitudes than they were in religion.

Let us examine the tenets of this Calvinistic theology, which was so dominant in the early cultural life of our nation. It derived its name from the Reformation leader, John Calvin, whose primary emphasis was on the sovereignty of God. In Calvin's concept, not kings and parliaments, but God ruled the universe. God's will was and is the basis of everything that exists. Even the (good) laws of man are the embodiment of His will.

This emphasis on the will of God played an important part in the colonists' strong determination to win in their cause against almost insurmountable odds, and gave them a strong sense of security in their tremulous world.

Man, said Calvin, being unable to lift himself, was ever in humility accepting Christ and throwing himself back on the mercy of God. No matter how lofty or humble the person, every life became an immensely important life when it was God-dominated and God-guided. Out of this concept came the strict morality of our Puritanical ances-

107

tors; here were emphasized the elemental virtues of reverence, sobriety, chastity, honesty, frugality, and industry.

God was not a casual acquaintance to whom the sentimental, well-meaning colonial "Kiwanian" could come with a wave of the hand or a slap on the back. The Calvinist could not regard so lightly the majesty and holiness of God.

The Calvinist studied his Bible and took from it an abhorrence of sensuous sin, of any form of excess, of deception and greed, and thus produced that rugged character which made him appear unduly stern to others.

Emphasizing that men may serve God in the market place as well as in the monastery, Calvin gave to Christianity a new sense of stewardship. By stressing the dignity and worth of honest labor and the wealth derived therefrom, and by giving his approval to the economic productivity of that wealth prudently invested, he laid the philosophic and ethical foundations for the modern industrial order, which, in turn, gave impetus to the rising middle class which is now the backbone of American social and economic life.

But Calvin also had a deep insight into the perils of prosperity. He believed that because people get intoxicated by prosperity, times of want were sent to bring them to their senses. He organized, nerved, and disciplined the human will to the uttermost, and in sobriety and labor taught men the individualism which is the basis of freedom.

On these Calvinistic views and principles, then, our forefathers builded, and builded well. "Calvinistic in inspiration and Puritan in essence," says Clinton Rossiter in

Seedtime of the Republic (Harcourt, Brace, 1953), "the great dissenting churches helped breed a new person, and this man, multiplied millions of times over, was to give American democracy its peculiar flavor. In its best aspects and moments Protestantism was a main source of these great political principles of American democracy: freedom of thought and expression, separation of church and state, local self-government, higher law, constitutionalism, the American Mission, and the free individual" (p. 40).

These principles have sustained us in war and peace. While at times we may have wavered from their truth and power, they have always risen to convict us.

The bitter truth is that we are always in danger of losing them. This is especially true in periods of national tension, war, and economic stress and strain. The departure from these standards is always most conspicuous after a great war, with its attendant decline.

We all know these periods of national strain. We remember the 1920's, which took us through the Jazz Age and up to an era of cynicism and agnosticism in higher education. In the 30's we suffered a great depression and witnessed the rise of a soft socialism. In the 40's we were at war, subjected to the strains that war brings to play on human emotion and personal character. We have been again through the whole round of the sins that John Calvin condemned, and we have lost the God our ancestor knew and worshiped.

We assumed new gods, or took a comfortable, irreverent view of the God of our fathers. We emphasized God's fatherhood, but not His majesty and holiness and justice. We listened to the anti-religionist in his effort to debunk Biblical faith, and our characters became the weaker for it.

In too many of us the virtue of chastity has been displaced by a ready surrender to the sins of the flesh. As for temperance and moderation, we have covered the gamut of experiment from an attempt at absolute legal prohibition to extreme intemperance and immoderation. Industry and frugality have been neglected, denounced, and discouraged, while making money by hook or crook has become the chief ambition of men. Honesty, for too many, has become no more than compliance with outward propriety. Honor is measured by the standard that right is what you can get away with. Nothing is wrong if you are not caught at it. Meanwhile, our homes have been disintegrating. Infidelity is rampant.

American culture, as our forefathers knew it, has so deteriorated in our lifetime that discriminating men with a knowledge of history have seriously pondered how long we can survive. Good and honorable men have prayed for a national moral resurgence and spiritual awakening on a very wide scale.

Always there remains amongst a great and good people a "remnant" faithful to the foundation principles of its greatness. Somehow or other, despite all their wickedness and wandering, Americans—when true to themselves—can never get very far away from God. The life of this Republic was cradled in the faith that God presides over His universe, and that nations and men in the end are accountable to Him. By His providence the nation came into being, and in His spirit it has become great. When Americans depart from the faith in God that created them, and the practice of His presence which strengthens them, and obedience to His will which guides them, then they are no longer truly Americans.

We cannot expect pagans to do what must be done at this hour if we are to recover the foundations of our greatness. Only committed men and women can do this. Others, let us hope, will be infused and empowered by contact with those whose souls are rekindled. If we have not yet come to understand that we must return in a very real and earnest way to the basic principles of American life as they are expressed in evangelical Christianity, we are not yet aware of the meaning of these days.

Let us look back now to that sturdy pioneer of the American frontier and reassess the American of today. The pioneer had his axe, his gun, and his Bible; he had few possessions, but he had rich spiritual endowments. Out of the wilderness before him he carved the vast empire that has become modern America.

From Vermont to Florida, this man built a nation incomparable in all history and today the envy of the world. No wonder men look longingly from afar on America as a refuge for the despairing, an asylum for the outcast, and a promise of that better world that is yet to be.

It is not enough to say that the American has produced all this simply because of the presence of vast natural resources secured against all enemies by wide ocean frontiers

111

and friendly neighbors. Other nations have had richer natural resources, and for a longer period of time. *The American succeeded because of his spirit—the spirit of the free man, derived from his religious faith.*

In some this faith was intimate and personal, the very essence of their being; in others, a less conscious Christian experience, but nevertheless an attitude of life derived from the climate and culture produced principally by evangelical Christianity. Even those who do not belong to the church have caught something of the spirit which the church produced.

Today's American no longer carries the axe, the gun, and the Bible. His axe has become America's gigantic industrial machine, and the world sees that. His gun has become America's powerful armament, and the world knows it well. His Book is pouring forth the light of a new awakening, *and the world must see that.*

To be worthy of our heritage, competent for new tasks, and builders of the new world, the light of that Book must shine through American lives so brightly at home that it will illumine the dark places of all mankind.

~~~~~~

CHAPTER VI

"The Ramparts We Watch"

Some years ago a motion picture called "The Ramparts We Watch" portrayed a great nation responding with vitality and vision to an historic emergency. It was a spectacle to warm the heart, stir the emotions, and rekindle the patriotic flame which burns in every American breast.

At this moment, when civilization is gasping for its breath, we need to reclaim the truth that the ramparts of our national life are not only our shores, our farms, our cities, and our factories, but also something much less physical and tangible.

A favorite indoor sport of foreign analysts of American life, and often the theme of visiting preachers from abroad, is condemning American materialism, which apparently is the only aspect of America they are able to see. They visit our big cities, gaze at our skyscrapers and factories, note our automobiles, television sets, and refrigerators, accept our hospitality and generous welcome, unabashedly accept a munificent fee or honorarium (the like of which they would never receive in their own land) and fail to see beyond this bounty the creative spirit and the industrial ingenuity which has produced the high standard of living in America. They fail to absorb the spiritual atmosphere which molded the character of America. To conclude that all this magnitude of production was motivated by a crass materialism and shallow spirit is to miss the very essence of the American way of life.

More important than our sea lanes or airways, our economic resources, industrial power, and military efficiency, the ramparts which give us real security rest in the character of our people, in the nature of our liberty, in the sanctity and stability of the home, and in the divine mission of the Church.

Our first defense inevitably turns on the character of our people. It was a people of strong character who built this nation, and only a strong people can be trusted with our great powers, privileges, and responsibilities.

One has only to read the history of early New England, Virginia, and the Middle Atlantic settlements to be impressed by this fact. Brought up on fundamental tenets of reference, industry, frugality, chastity, sobriety, and honesty, they were a sturdy lot, with a strong sense of righteousness, justice, and personal integrity. Theirs was a stern philosophy, but it was Christian and it was not weak.

114

The earlier settlers, the English, Scotch, Irish and Scotch-Irish, were succeeded by freedom-seeking French, by Germans fleeing Prussian militarism, by Italians, Scandinavians, Russians, and others who had caught the vision of a land of liberty and opportunity. Most of them lived under the dominion of a God who was to them the Sovereign Ruler of a moral universe; they felt that they were responsible in their individual and social conduct to that kind of a God. They were refugees from political and religious oppression, but they were not fugitives from high moral concepts and disciplined religious living. There was something noble and great in them which we need in our day if we are to emerge from the present chaos as a people worthy of survival. We need that quality today which makes character a firm alloy, compounded of human strength, divine grace, kindness, firmness, gentleness, ruggedness, and a determination to live for and to enforce justice.

As we have said before, only men of majestic character can be trusted with their own destinies. The character of our people is the first rampart of the nation, over which we must keep watch.

The second rampart is a corollary of the first. It turns on the kind of liberty we have inherited, and on how greatly we cherish it.

Liberty, as we understand it, did not come by accident. It came as the gift of God in time. The source of our liberty, according to the Hebrew-Christian tradition, is in God's creative act. The freedom we know is not something

115

we have achieved or something granted to us by a government; it is the gift of God to man as part of his creation. Governments may acknowledge that freedom, but they cannot bestow it; and no power on earth has the right to take away our freedom under God.

This kind of freedom has been possible only because we kept alive the faith that produced it. This kind of freedom will exist only so long as we have the character to express it in our personal and national life.

The price of liberty is the assumption of personal responsibility for one's own well-being and a measure of responsibility for that of his fellows. It means participation in the privileges of a democratic Christian society. Our freedoms of worship, speech, vote, and press are not worth much if we ourselves ever come to the place where we have no God to worship. The liberty to have many religious faiths, many political parties, and great economic resources cannot be long continued if we lack the spirit of the Lord in our lives, which makes us employ these privileges worthily.

As heirs of this tradition, we must always remember that our freedom, as God's gift, is not freedom to do as we please, but only as God pleases; that freedom ends where it infringes on the common good or the rights of another whose freedom is also bestowed on him by God.

We cannot say too frequently or with too much emphasis that the thing which is distinctive in our national life is our faith in God—a God who, while being the God of all men, becomes in a special sense the God of those who accept His purpose and obey His law. The only true freedom is

116

freedom under God—freedom by submission to the Higher Authority.

We do an ill thing if we try to have the fruits of our democracy and neglect the roots. There are many people today who hold that the Church is unnecessary, that they do not have to join an organized church to be respectable and worthy citizens. I meet men every day who are eager to tell me that "grandfather was an elder, and Uncle John was a deacon," but that they themselves do not belong to any church or share in the responsibility for promoting its welfare. They do, however, desire the respectable offices of the Church. They want their children to be baptized and married under the auspices of the Church. They want the parson to open the service-club program with prayer, to serve on the civic welfare committee, to recruit solicitors from his church membership for the Red Cross campaigns. When death invades their homes they would like to have the word of God's comfort uttered in the presence of the dead—though they have not often paused to read or hear them before. These good folks, participating in the Church-sponsored fruits of our common life, do attend church regularly—regularly every Easter Sunday.

The tragedy of all this is that these people are frequently the most anxious about the security of America and the most zealous in opposing the Communist peril. Yet they forsake and neglect our strongest bulwark against this menacing force. They fail to see that their grandfathers whom they so much admire were admirable men and violent in opposition to totalitarian tyranny mainly be-

117

cause they worked at the religion which their grandsons so easily neglect. Our land is filled with men and women who willingly join fifty-seven varieties of clubs, fraternities, and lodges, and give mind and heart to many of them, but who neglect and fail to support the one institution that has given substance and meaning to the life of America.

Of course, such people do not *have* to join the Church. They do not have to join the Church if they do not want to live in a Christian nation. They do not have to join the Church if they no longer believe in the values it conserves. They do not need to join the Church if they no longer want to promote the culture derived primarily from the Church.

The principal reason for joining the Church of Christ should always be one of commitment to our Lord Jesus Christ and an earnest desire to bear common witness with others to the Gospel of redeeming love, to share in the Church's fellowship, and to be strengthened by its prayers. Appreciation of our way of life, and of the sources of our liberty is not the highest motive for joining the Church, but it cannot be said with too great urgency to those who hope for a rebirth of patriotism that one of the most patriotic things an American can do today is to become a living part of the Church of God.

Another rampart we must make secure is the home. Our pioneer homes made our nation great. They were places of industry, piety, and democracy. The barn or wagonshed, for the men and boys, and the kitchen for women and girls, provided centers of industry. The home was a sanctuary in which the family became a congregation regularly honoring the word of God and worshiping the eternal Lord of Life. The dining-table and the fireside assembly were arenas of political discussion—the prep schools of democracy. The father was prophet, priest and king—prophet in teaching the word of truth, priest in leading his family in many a religious exercise, and king because he enforced the moral law. And the home was linked to the Church by the institution of the family pew.

What has happened to all this? Many homes are falling apart for the want of a moral and spiritual foundation. Sacred vows are repudiated, infidelity is condoned, contracts are dissolved, emotions damaged, minds dwarfed, child development is warped, and personality destroyed. Moral and spiritual guidance is minimized, if not neglected entirely. Religion has become a domestic option. The Bible, while physically present, is too often an unexplored volume.

Family life no longer possesses its interpreting and unifying strength. When the family gathers it is not at the family altar or even at the fireside, but in front of the television screen, where each contends with the other for his favorite show. Home has come to be a place to which one goes to get ready to go somewhere else. The living room is the distance between dining-room table and the front door. Home is a dormitory by night and a commissary by day. That is why we are all the more grateful for the Christian homes we yet behold. But something disastrous is happening to the sanctity and stability of the average American home.

The family pew is almost a relic of bygone days. How is it that parents will let their children sit through double-feature motion pictures which are often emotionally injurious, but will not insist that they participate in the religious double-feature of Sunday school and church?

And what hope have we for the future when so many of our parents make no place whatever for religion in their own lives, or in those of their children? Recently nearly thirty per cent of the students in one of our high schools were so uninformed in religion that they could not even indicate a religious preference.

Will it require a major disaster to persuade us of a truth that the ministers of religion have been preaching with heartbreaking passion—that unless we re-establish life on a spiritual foundation our future generations are doomed? A blatant and blasphemous paganism and a disastrous materialistic philosophy will assume its damning dominion over American life and noble living will have vanished unless that re-establishment comes—and soon!

Many a man among us, however, is beginning to have a haunting feeling that he would like to recover what he has lost. With Strickland Gillilan, in *The Cry of An Alien*, he would say:

I'm an alien—I'm an alien to the faith my mother taught me:
I'm a stranger to the comfort that my "Now I lay me"
    brought me,
To the Everlasting Arms that held my father when he died.
I have spent a lifetime seeking things I spurned when I had
    found them:
I have fought and been rewarded in full many a winning
    cause:

But I'd yield them all—fame, fortune, and the pleasures that
    surround them
For a little of the faith that made my mother what she was.

I was born where God was closer to His children and
    addressed them
With the tenderest of messages through bird and tree and
    bloom:
I was bred where people stretched upon the velvet sod to rest
    them,
Where the twilight's benediction robbed the coming night of
    gloom.
But I've built a wall between me and the simple life behind me:
I have coined my heart and paid it for the fickle world's
    applause:
Yet I think His hand would fumble through the voiceless dark
    and find me
If I only had the faith that made my mother what she was.

When the great world came and called me, I deserted all
    to follow:
Never knowing, in my dazedness, I had slipped my hand
    from His—
Never noting, in my blindness, that the bauble fame was
    hollow,
That the gold of wealth was tinsel, as I since have learned it is.
I have spent a lifetime seeking things I've spurned when I
    have found them:
I have fought and been rewarded in full many a petty cause,
But I'd take them all—fame, fortune and the pleasures that
    surround them,
And exchange them for the faith that made my mother what
    she was.

(By courtesy of B. S. Gillilan)

The faith that made that kind of mother was faith in the Bible as the living Word of God, faith in God as the Sovereign Ruler of life, faith in Christ as Saviour and Lord, and faith in His living presence—the Master of our homes, our market places, and our legislative halls.

We must also maintain as the chief rampart of all the Christian Church in its pristine vitality. In the Church's life and message is the solid foundation of every other rampart. "Other foundation have we none than that which is in Jesus Christ," and in the apostles. Many a man who declares his willingness to fight for democracy has not yet begun to live for its undergirding organism—the Church.

The Church must have the allegiance of men who say they believe in it if our kind of democracy is to prevail. If men are to be trusted with their own destinies they must be the kind of men produced by the Christian Gospel.

When Albert Einstein observed the rising threat of totalitarianism in Germany he said he expected its chief opposition to come first from the press and from men of letters. When these groups were strangely tractable Einstein placed his hope in the universities, in the liberal minds of discriminating scholars; but these men were docile and submissive, too. Where, then, should he look? Only in the churches did he behold men of valiant spirit making vigorous resistance to the Nazi movement. And he came to respect the Church as he had never respected it before.

In much of the world the Church is a minority move-

ment amid a vast paganism, yet it does hold the answer to
the needs of our world. It is not a new movement. It is
rooted in antiquity and anchored in eternity and it has the
stability of the ages. The Church came by men, and it has
human qualities, but it is not an institution of men. It
originated in an act of God. It stakes its life on the first
words of Scripture: "In the beginning God . . ."

Sometimes the Church is unpopular because it understands our sin and righteousness too well, and because
sometimes it points at us with the words, "Thou art the
man." Sinners and hypocrites there may be within the
Church, but they are people who know where their need
is satisfied. Knowing all the weakness alleged against the
Church, I know of no other institution keeping alive such
a genuine sense of God and high values. It is a living
organism, not of those who are perfect, but of those who
have found a perfect Lord; not of those who are sinless,
but of those who have found a Saviour from sin; not of
completely holy men, but of men who worship a Holy God.

The Church is not a company carrying a bunch of keys
to unlock the doors to all our problems, but a people with
a master key to the whole of life. It is not a society discussing truth, but a fellowship of the redeemed of God,
presenting the Truth in the person of Christ her Lord. In
spite of persecution from without and secularism and division within, the Church is still a "colony of Heaven," and
it is yet the "salt of the earth." It is of God.

Out of this revelation from God came our civil liberties,
our schools, our public libraries, our hospitals, our free

press, our cherished democracy. These will survive only if their real source, the Church, has the complete devotion of the American people. It is only "where the spirit of the Lord is" that we can nourish and conserve the kind of life that makes us both great and good.

CHAPTER VII

A Time for Intolerance

One Sunday I preached on "The Inescapable Truth"—a sermon about the Truth as it is in the person of Jesus Christ. The press across the country carried excerpts of various passages, and mail poured in. Here is one letter written in response to one quotation from the sermon; it comes from a city in the far West:

Dear Stupid Dr. Elson:

Do not try to impress the public of Washington, D.C., with your false light of Presbyterianism; Sir Mussoline, Sir Hitler, and Sir Stalin—they were great men, men of great wisdom, men of God—You have no reason, no intelligence, in any way, shape, or form, to stand before an audience of high culture, to make a false statement against God people. . . . I am a man, "a servant of the most high" and I will suggest to you, stop

125

preaching false doctrine to the public, and go to work on pick and shovel, that you may feel better, and this earth will be more clean.

Sincerely yours

"The Man of Wisdom"

There is obviously here an element of abnormality. This pathological "Man of Wisdom" is in need of a physician. But not all who write such letters are sick. Some are sane, but woefully wrong. When Christian truth is proclaimed, it evokes the response of untruth. I am beginning to wonder whether we have not been too tolerant of such bigotry and untruth.

One of the great dangers of our age is our easy tolerance. Ancient Israel had this temptation, too—the temptation to "put other Gods before Yahweh," to add to the historic faith in such a tolerant manner as to produce a syncretistic worship. The tendency in ancient Israel was toward an easy and tolerant liberalism, while the great prophets were perpetual protestants against this tendency.

In those parts of the Israelitish population where tolerance won, vital religion perished because of the lack of vigorous protestations in crucial times. Dr. D. Elton Trueblood points out that the ten lost tribes of Israel were not so much lost, in the sense of migration, as that they were lost in the sense that they ceased to be a people conscious of the unique witness. Thank God, the prophets, by their intolerance, came to the faith. And that faith gave us Jesus Christ.

Jesus came out of that Jewish tradition—a tradition accustomed to the rise of prophets who by being critical of their times were productive of new times. The so-called narrow men of Israel saved the faith and the nation.

Our Lord was kind and he was compassionate, but there were times when He demonstrated that tolerance is not always a virtue. Of some things He would be tolerant; some other things He would not tolerate at all. So you behold Him in His last week upsetting the money tables and driving the money-changers from the temple of God.

There is no greater distortion of Christian principle than the prevalent assumption that the Christian must be tolerant at all times. To suppose that tolerance of everyone and everything at all times and in all places is a virtue is to misunderstand the nature of the Christian life. There are times when Christians must be tolerant. But there are other times when Christians dare not be tolerant. To be tolerant under all circumstances is to blunt the sharp-edged convictions and to dissipate spiritual vitality.

The Christian will have a hospitable mind for other men's ideas; but can he be tolerant of falsehood?

The Christian will be tolerant of other human beings; but can he be tolerant of the evil some men manifest?

The Christian will be tolerant of other faiths; but must he be tolerant of those practices in other faiths which, if tolerated, would destroy his own faith?

The Christian will be tolerant in his advocacy of free speech; but must he be tolerant of those subversive forces

127

which use our free speech to seek power which, if achieved, would destroy free speech?

The Christian will be tolerant of other people's opinions as expressed in a free press; but must he be tolerant of those who exploit the free press for achieving personal power, or for the assassination of character?

The Christian will be tolerant of those whose moral standards differ from his own; but must he be tolerant of those whose scandalous conduct violates Christian morality, destroys American idealism, and harms our nation's influence abroad?

The Christian will have a basic tolerance of other races, which is the very essence of Christianity; but must he be tolerant of those who exploit variations from his Christian standard solely to achieve political ambitions?

The Christian will be tolerant of those who differ from him in their opinions concerning political philosophy, economic theory, and even public morality; but must he be tolerant of opinions which undercut our culture, violate decency, and sow the seeds of social collapse?

No! There are limits to tolerance. There are times when tolerance is not a virtue, but a vice. This is a lesson we Protestants need to learn. At times our tolerance has been our weakness; it could be our undoing. When we have become too tolerant, we have sometimes lost our convictions. And with our convictions lost, we lose our hold upon men.

When Brotherhood Week comes around each year, and I am invited to speak on the same platform with my

Roman Catholic and Jewish colleagues, I am always glad to participate. Whatever we can do to demonstrate our common allegiances within the framework of American life has a constructive influence. It is usual during Brotherhood Week to discuss the great truths we hold in common. A more useful purpose might be served, it seems to me, if at times we were to define the points in which we differ, and to assert that which makes us unique. Tolerance does not mean acquiescence in another's faith nor diluting one's own; and our brotherhood might be furthered at times if we really sharpened our differences and recognized wherein each of us is different. To see another as he sees himself is to be a better human brother. To help each other preserve his uniqueness could conceivably be a great contribution to brotherhood. At any rate, in being tolerant we must not forfeit the convictions which give us virility and substance.

At all times the Christian must be charitable, but charity and tolerance are not the same thing. Some of the most virile churches have been those which might be said to be the most intolerant, and some of our sturdiest Christians are those thought by others to be a bit narrow. Some of our forceful organizations are slightly intolerant: for example, the intemperate temperance societies whose members keep our moral distinctions sharpened!

Tolerance can become a weakness. When the Roman Catholic priest censors a person because he absents himself from the rites of the church and imposes upon him a severe penance, he is called a good and faithful priest of the

Church. But when the governing body of a Protestant Church proposes to suspend from membership a person who has not darkened the doors of the Church for a quarter of a century, that governing body is said to be "intolerant." When the priest says, "You must attend mass each week or fail to be in a state of grace . . ." or, to put it more bluntly, "You must go to church or you go to hell," the priest is called a good Catholic. But when I say, "You cannot be a good Christian at all unless you have disciplined habits of worship," and suggest that absence from the common worship and fellowship of Christ's Church is in the end disastrous to you, I am said to be intolerant.

Toward what are we to be tolerant? Are we to be tolerant of spiritual indifference? Are we to be tolerant of shallow theology? Are we to be tolerant of religious apathy?

Tolerance is a virtue much of the time, but it is not a virtue all of the time. Tolerance may indeed become a vice and lead to our decay.

There are some things for which we must stand. There are also some things against which we must stand. There must be a ruggedness in our Christian faith which competing faiths and external pressures cannot destroy.

There are some things from which the Christian must not deviate. There must be muscle and backbone in the Christian character, and there are times which call for a moral defiance in the heart.

"Be strong in the Lord and in the power of his might," was not meant for softies, nor was the call, "Stand immovable, always abounding in the works of the Lord," intended for weaklings.

There are some things which simply cannot be tolerated. Truth can never be tolerant toward falsehood; morality cannot be tolerant toward immorality; Christianity cannot be tolerant toward paganism.

Let us endeavor to keep the virtuous kind of tolerance. Let us endeavor to stand resolutely for the convictions we most assuredly believe, exercising charity toward those with whom we differ. Let us ask for ourselves nothing we would deny to other races or to other faiths. But simply to be tolerant toward everything for the sake of tolerance is highly dangerous to our religion and our way of life.

This is also a time for intolerance of those who abuse our American freedom. When we understand how we got our freedom and how precious it is to us, we will not tolerate its abuse.

The Christian must be intolerant of those who act as though freedom means license to do as one pleases. To be free does not mean that we have no limitations. I can never be free in the sense that I can do all things at all times as my whims and fancies dictate. I am limited by my self-respect. I am limited by my sense of duty. I am limited by my consideration for others. I am limited by my sense of decency. I am limited by the sanctions and traditions of my community. I am limited by my neighbor's welfare. I am limited by my personal sense of honor.

Because I belong to others, my freedom is limited. I have a wife and that limits my freedom. I have a home and family and that limits my freedom. I have a church and parishioners and that limits my freedom. I live in a community with other people and that limits my freedom.

You, too, have limitations. You belong to the Church and that limits your freedom. You are a citizen of the United States and your freedom is limited by the freedom of other citizens.

We all belong to Christ and that limits our freedom. We are mastered by Him, commanded by Him, and our destiny is in His hands.

Freedom brings with it deep loyalties. Freedom demands disciplines. Freedom requires personal responsibility. It is time to be intolerant of that cheap conception of freedom which says that you can do as you please.

This is a time for the Church of Jesus Christ to be intolerant of everything which attempts to deprive it of its unique reality as the instrument of God upon the earth. It is a time to assert the distinctive nature of the "body of Christ," which is the Church.

The Church is not a jolly social club. Of the early Christians, it was written, "These are they which have turned the world upside down."

The Church is not a Sunday morning lecture forum. It is a fellowship of redeemed sinners, of whom it has been written, "Behold, how they love one another."

The Church is not a political debating society; it is a "colony of heaven," the concrete and living evidence of Jesus Christ on earth.

It is time for the Church, deriving its very life from

132

God, to be intolerant of any agency, governmental or otherwise, which endeavors to deprive it of its inherent authority and its divine mission. It stakes its faith on the historic doctrine that God is the Sovereign Lord and Ruler of all life. The Church, when faithful to its Lord, is thus the medium of the voice of God, and it stands in judgment on all life, including governments; for the God of the Church, who is the God of history, is above and beyond all human societies, including the State. Therefore the Church, when true to its Lord, is to be judged only by the one Divine Judge.

In America the Church has cultivated our kind of liberty and has produced some of our greatest patriots. Not a few of them have been clergymen. And the clergy today yield to no other citizens in their patriotic allegiance. The ministers of religion today, as individual citizens, gladly accept all the responsibility and privileges of citizenship. Their contribution to the total life of the nation is rich and meaningful. As individual citizens, they are ready to co-operate with every effort to strengthen and maintain our national foundations. As individual citizens, but not as a vocational class, they are for the most part ready to participate in every positive and constructive movement for inculcating in Americans a better understanding of our way of life and protecting that way of life from the forces which would subvert or destroy it. Therefore, as individual citizens but not as a vocational class, when true to their heritage, they welcome honest scrutiny of their own lives by competent investigative agencies.

133

For if the life of a minister of religion is not lived in the open and if he cannot be trusted he cannot lead. If a minister of religion cannot lead in the things of the spirit, on which our life is so dependent, then he must vacate his leadership to someone who can lead. But the truth of the matter is that there is no body of men more dedicated to God and as thoroughly loyal to the standards of American democracy as the ministers of the Church of Christ. Were they not so loyal, and did they love their country less, they would not seek in so many ways to keep her true to her foundations, to correct her mistakes, and to urge full use of her opportunities to serve and uplift the whole world.

Every minister worthy of the name and worthy of the ordination with which he has been invested has already been investigated by a higher Source than any government can offer. His life has been laid bare before Almighty God. His motives, his purposes, his ambitions in life, all have been subordinated to the eternal God. As in few other callings, the minister has been scrutinized doctrinally, intellectually, morally, and spiritually by the authorities of his church. Both as the examiner and the examined, he is accustomed to investigations.

It is because he is familiar with investigations and examinations that he knows the value of competent and trustworthy investigations and the peril of unworthy and ulterior probings.

Every individual's life should be open to scrutiny. With proper safeguards to freedom of thought and conscience, the clergy as individual citizens are ready now, as always, to participate in every responsible effort for the purification of our national life in consonance with the Church's fundamental conviction that "God alone is Lord of the conscience."

When ministers as a group are made special targets of inquisitions, on the premise that they are promoters of disloyalty, they naturally are concerned about the motives and methods of inquisitors.

When the leaders of the Church are slandered and misrepresented by political charlatans for the purposes of their own political advancement, it is time for the Church to become intolerant of the charlatan, who is in every sense subversive and a saboteur. The clergy would give general approbation to President Eisenhower's statement of July 10, 1953:

If there be found any among us, whatever his calling, guilty of treasonous action against the State, let him legally and properly be convicted and punished. This applies to every person, lay or clergy.

The churches of America are citadels of our faith in individual freedom and human dignity. This faith is the living source of all our spiritual strength. And this strength is our matchless armor in our world-wide struggle against the forces of Godless tyranny and oppression.

The time for intolerance of the forces which would destroy both our Church and our cherished nation is at hand. As we have pointed out earlier, Communism is not a Christian heresy but a new religion of salvation, calling

135

for the complete dedication of men and women and youth, and commanding all their resources. This new religion, evoking the complete allegiance of its followers, and possessed of evangelistic fervor and crusading passion, is out to win converts and to make the world over in its own fashion.

There is only one way for us Christians to meet such a force. That is to know what our faith is, to cling tenaciously to our own convictions, and to remain committed without deviation to our own Lord. Then, as was true with the Early Church, we must outlive, outlove, outlast, and, if need be, outdie the Communists.

We follow a Christ who loved and served people—all kinds of people. He loved the sinner, but never compromised with sin. He was never diverted from the supreme purpose of fulfilling His Father's will. He was intolerant of hypocrisy, intolerant of sacrilege, intolerant of moral compromise.

I plead for a clearer understanding of our faith, a firmer commitment to Christ, and a holy intolerance of anything which keeps us from the exaltation of our Lord.

~~~~~~

CHAPTER VIII

Maintaining Spiritual Disciplines

Nothing is more important today than that we as a nation recapture the basic disciplines of our faith. In times of stress—periods of persecution or war, for instance—we discipline ourselves willingly and rigidly. But when better days return we forget all that, get back to being lazy and careless again as quickly as possible, and forego the disciplines of emergency which have made us strong in the crisis.

Faced on the one side by moral deterioration and on the other by an upsurge of moral aspiration and spiritual revival, what can the servants of God do to meet the challenge of this day?

With the prophet of old, we must cry out to God, "Speak, Lord, for thy servant heareth." For our lives cannot speak to this generation unless they carry a message—an authentic message which emanates from a Godly life.

And our lives cannot be effective conveyors of God's message to mankind except they be disciplined lives, totally committed to His purposes.

Nearly a year before Pearl Harbor I took out my diary and wrote in it three vows which I want to share with you now.

The first vow is this: I promised to maintain my spiritual disciplines steadfastly and at all costs. I had noted men in civilian life and in the military who had neglected this, and their lives had been tragic. I resolved to keep my disciplines of devotions, not in a dutiful fashion, but out of the love of God, come what might.

Secondly, I vowed that I would keep alive whatever creative powers God had given me. As a preacher, this meant for me to keep my homiletical instincts sharpened, to write new sermons constantly, to give fresh talks every time I was called on to speak. I must confess that some of the things I wrote during the war were chiefly for that purpose.

Thirdly, I vowed to keep bitterness and resentment out of my life. Jealousy of position, envy of rank, resentment over another man's assignment—all of these things could be toxins which would poison my whole system, until I could become a shriveled, narrow, little soul unfit for my high calling of the ministry.

Once I had put these resolutions in my diary, I made a discovery. I discovered that if I kept the first of these vows I had no difficulty with the other two. If I kept my spiritual disciplines I found my creative powers sharpened. I discovered fresh ideas for sermons clamoring for expression. And I also discovered that if I prayed as I should and loved God as I ought, there was then no room for jealousy and resentment. Then, when some other chaplain was struggling to keep his soul on fire, I was able to point him to these simple vows which had helped me.

In the military chaplaincy, as in the civilian ministry, there were administrative duties which tested the spirit more sorely than did the more intimate ministry to the spiritual needs of our young men in khaki. If a chaplain's only ambition was to keep mail moving from the "in" basket to the "out" basket, to post an accurate Council Book or to prepare an impressive report, important as this was, he might have a secular influence, but men would see only the ordered office and miss the living Christ.

A clergyman may even go about spiritual duties in a secular manner; his religious work may itself be performed in an irreligious attitude. The problem for the clergyman, and for those earnest Christians who come to him for help turns on maintaining his spiritual disciplines at all times and under all circumstances.

How can we keep our souls in this kind of world? A text which we might keep before us would be the words of the Apostle Paul in II Corinthians 5:14: "The love of Christ controls us" (RSV). To surrender to God, to know Him, to love Him, to be loved by Him, to be kept by Him —that is the rôle of the Christian in this day, as it was in Paul's day.

To be thus controlled by the love of Christ we must have the discipline of soul scrutiny. By this I do not mean morbid introspection. I do not mean digging up past moral failures, ethical compromises and sins, and then caressing them. Corpses never smell nice, and moral failures are always ugly to look at. By soul-scrutiny I mean conscience-testing, conscience-reading, that is, evaluating one's own life in comparison with the life of Christ, who is the Supreme Pattern.

Some branches of the Church provide the medium of the Confessional for this purpose. But what I am talking about is not thus limited. What one needs is an accurate and conscientious assessment of his life, to ask whether or not he has clean hands, a clean heart, and a clean mind. It comes by the application of spiritual tests and measurements. It may come by self-evaluation if that is utterly ruthless and thorough.

Whether it is obligatory or voluntary, the soul periodically must find itself calling out: "Search me, O God, and know my heart; try me and know my thoughts and see if there be any evil in me, and lead me in the way everlasting."

The second discipline which we must keep, and keep at all costs, is the discipline of quietness. Despite the environment, and even amid turmoil, it is possible for the soul to be so disciplined that there is always an inner center of quietness. The things we must know and the things we must utter come only to the quiet heart.

The discipline of quietness is not easy for Americans,

is it? We are always in a hurry. We live by a "green-light" psychology. We keep rushing hither and yon, only to watch everyone else rush hither and yon.

> I do not know, I do not care
> How far it is to anywhere;
> I only know that where I'm not
> Is always the alluring spot.

This is the American mood. Somebody said that he had explored the anatomy of a young American to discover where the principal callous was to be found. After a very careful exploration, the callous was found—neither on the right hand nor on the left, as might have been true of his father's anatomy, but on the sole of his right foot at the precise point where this foot touched the accelerator of his automobile. That callous, too, is a symbol of America's temperament.

Life is built on the principle of alternation: rest and work, quietness and expression. Jesus studied ten years for every year of expression and prayed ten hours for every hour of preaching. We simply must be quiet if we are to be effective. "The Seven Storied Mountain," written by a young Trappist monk may not be the answer to this problem for all of us, but certainly its popularity is symptomatic of a deep universal longing for quietness and meditation and at least occasional recess from the uproar of the world.

We who are Christians must exercise the discipline of quietness. We may find it on a hillside, in a room at home, in a church, in a chapel, or in a sacrament, but find it and keep it we must.

The Bible says, "In quietness and confidence shall be our strength." And there is another phrase which says, "He giveth quietness." He it is who gives the quietness, but we are the people who must exercise the discipline of the quiet heart.

Also, there is the spiritual discipline of reading. Each of us should read carefully the devotional directives of his own church. But we must also expose ourselves to the spiritual literature of the ages. The Scriptures will come first, and the works of the mystics and saints will occupy a large place in our reading.

Someone has said that a book is not worth reading until it is fifty years old. Following this rule, we could miss all the modern mystics and the spiritual enrichment of many a modern writing destined for the "classics" of fifty years hence. On the other hand, if we read nothing but modern books we would miss the spiritual gold mines in Milton's *Paradise Lost* and Bunyan's *Pilgrim's Progress*—and the gold mines in a host of other "elderly" volumes.

There are some books which are to be read for intellectual expansion and some for mere recreation, but the most important books for us as Christians will be those read for the sake of the cultivation of the soul.

To these disciplines of soul-scrutiny, quietness, and purposeful reading—we would add a fourth, the discipline of prayer.

Some churches have a prescribed daily discipline of

prayer for their members, others allow them greater freedom in developing the life of prayer. Whatever the procedure a man establishes, he cannot neglect this primary source of power; everything turns on the spirit with which he approaches prayer, and no careless routine, no half-hearted approach will bring him to the throne of Grace. Only by hungering and thirsting after God, only by yearning to know and to do the will of God, only by meeting God at appointed times and places, will a man be fit for the challenges of today's living.

A great musician once said, "If I stop practicing for one day, I know it; for two days, my friends know it; for three days, the connoisseurs know it; and if I stop practicing for four days, the whole world knows it." So it is with prayer.

If we fail to pray we cannot conceal the fact. Cease to pray and we become moody, irritable, depressed. Fail to pray and our spiritual muscles shrink.

Physicians and ministers agree that there is important correlation between the health of the body and the health of mind and spirit. The laws of health which apply to the body apply also to the mind and the spirit.

Was it Dr. Fosdick who recently reminded us that "health is correspondence with environment—for body and for spirit alike"? Health of body depends on its correspondence with the environment of light and air. Let there be a lack of air and the lungs fail, a lack of light and the eyes fail. Health of mind, too, is correspondence with its environment, but its environment is the world of perception and ideas. Where there is no correspondence of mind and ideas the mind suffers distortions and blurs, and psychosis sets in. Health of the soul is correspondence with its environment, and the environment of the soul is God Himself.

In its highest form, prayer, of course, is communion. Disturb that correspondence, and the soul suffers. Prayer has its own rewards and every praying soul recognizes them—quickened faculties, clearer vision, steadier nerves, and reinforced personality.

People know whether or not we pray, and we will never do much for them or for God if we do not live the life of prayer.

Now, discipline is said to be the "ordered control of outward action and inward mood in accordance with a controlling purpose in life." The controlling purpose for us as Christians ought to be to glorify God in all that we do and say and think. We may fail in some areas; we cannot afford to fail in the discipline of prayer.

Our friends in the Salvation Army have a very suggestive phrase; that noble band of God's Army in the streets refers to devotional exercise as "knee drill." We must all be adept at knee drill.

No spiritual discipline is so earnestly needed as the discipline of group worship. One of the more distinctive features of Protestantism is that of "Common Worship." Common worship means participation by individuals in common or united expressions of worship. Thus, several major churches have guides to worship called "The Book of Common Worship," or "The Book of Common Order."

These provide for the orderly engagement of individual Christians in group worship.

This unique characteristic of Protestantism is made more pointed when contrasted with other theories of Divine worship. The devout Roman Catholic sees, in the basic service of his church a religious spectacle. He is a witness to a drama—the Sacrifice of the Mass, which is a reenactment of the atonement of Christ for the worshiper's sins. According to the precepts of this church, if he can view the drama in disciplined exercise of his personal faith, the action is then effective for his salvation. The action is something done for him rather than something which he does himself.

The Protestant who understands his own faith goes to church as something better than an observer; he is himself a participant in the "Common Worship." He enters into the action personally. He joins with others in a common witness. The action is not something done on his behalf; it is something which he does with others. With others, he sings, prays, reads, makes public confession, and hears the Word of God.

There is a vast distinction between an audience and a Christian church at worship. An audience is simply an assembly of "auditors" or "observers." As spectators, they have come to behold something. But a Christian church at worship is a corporate fellowship taking common or united action. By this common worship, God is approached and becomes real; and by the action there is the corporate proclamation of faith.

Common worship is more than the assembly of Christian

individuals offering individual expressions of worship. Common worship is the *collective and united* expression of the worshipers, which is more than the sum total of its participants. There is in it a "plus" factor. This sharing together as "participants" as distinguished from "observers" is one of the most distinctive features of the Protestant faith.

This is not always understood by some who presume to be Protestant. The individual who goes "church shopping," flitting from one church to another, enamored by the sensational preacher of the moment, becomes a sort of religious "bobby soxer"; he is "wowed" by every pulpit idol who comes along. This religious roving is hardly the highest or best expression of Christian devotion. Psychologically, it is the attitude of the theater-goer, who requires frequent change of play, rather than the genuine attitude of the committed participant in a true fellowship, sharing in a community of the spirit. However exhilarated these religious nomads may feel, they have only fleeting attachments to a procession of fascinating personalities and an insufficient dedication to their Lord. They are basically spectators and not participants in common worship.

Thirty years ago President Theodore Roosevelt called Americans to the discipline of corporate worship. The churchgoer, said Roosevelt,

may not hear a good sermon at church. But unless he is very unfortunate he will hear a sermon by a good man . . . and, besides, even if he does not hear a good sermon, the probabilities are that he will listen to and take part in reading some

146

beautiful passage from the Bible. . . . Moreover, he will probably take part in singing some good hymns. He will meet and nod to or speak to good quiet neighbors. Church attendance and church work of some kind mean both the cultivation of the habit of feeling some responsibility for others and the sense of braced moral strength which prevents the relaxation of one's fiber.

The Son of God subjected Himself to the disciplines of the Synagogue; His life showed the discipline of His regular worship in the house of God. He worshiped every Sabbath Day, "as was his custom," in what Winifred Kirkland has described as a "quarrelsome, sordid village synagogue," perhaps among gossips and hypocrites. Doubtless our Lord found much in the church of His day that wearied and vexed Him and revolted His sensibilities—the parade of righteousness by some of the religious leaders, and the "holier than thou" attitude of those who kept the minute regulations of the law, the narrow-minded little bigotries, the small dogmas made big and the big realities made small. How he hated—and later condemned—the feeble faith of His day!

Yet, despite all this, Jesus remained a faithful and true member of His church—loyal and regular in His attendance at worship, giving His whole life to its purposes. Here, as a lad, He came to know the Bible of His people; He learned to read it, memorized parts of it, and absorbed His favorite passages from Deuteronomy, Hosea, Isaiah, and the Psalter. Later these passages were the foundation of His preaching and the strength of His life. The Scriptures

147

were fulfilled in His life. He not only demonstrated the truths of the Scriptures; He drew upon them for help in His personal life—even on the Cross.

If He condemned the Synagogue, He did so from within and not from without—as one who had everything precious in life to gain from His Church, and one who could not abandon it without losing His own soul.

Looking at Jesus of Nazareth, noting His unvarying fidelity to the discipline of worship—who are we to suppose that we can get along without its worship, its fellowship, its God? We cannot be the Christians Jesus called us to be without being members of His Church, sharing in its activity, partaking of its sacraments, hearing its truths, being bound and controlled by its life.

If we would claim the forgiveness and the redemption and the "new life in Christ," His Church must claim us. There is no other way to keep the faith, and there is no worthy way to transmit that faith except by and through the Church. The Church exists not as an option for the Christian but as the imperative in his life. The Church is the living body of Christ among men, the instrument of His salvation for the world.

We are not connoisseurs, but crusaders. We are not passengers, but pilgrims. Either we have been redeemed by faith in Christ and identify ourselves with the redeemed in the Church, or redemption by faith in Christ has lost its meaning. There is no "beloved community" without "the beloved." There is literally no salvation outside the Church. Nothing is permanently salvaged alone, or con-

148

served in isolation. Only when joined with the "saints in light" is there growth and power.

Some years ago Ernest Dousett wrote a book in which he pictured a Scottish minister making a call on a Highland family who attended his kirk in an endeavor to induce in them a deeper commitment to God. As he approached the house he noticed the well-kept garden, the finely painted fence, and the clean, neat appointments of the home. He knocked at the door and was greeted by the lady of the home. Lifting his hat, he inquired in his simple, direct manner, "Does Jesus live here?"

Momentarily taken aback, she remained silent.

He pressed his question again, and asked, "Does Jesus live here?"

Not knowing what to say, she fled to the rear of the house, while the minister replaced his hat and went quietly on his way.

When her husband reached home in the evening, she said to him, "John, the minister of our kirk has been here and he asked a curious question. He wanted to know if Jesus lived here."

"Well," said John with some irritation, "did you not tell him that we go to the kirk on the Lord's Day and that we put our money in the offering?"

"Aye, aye, John, that I was minded to say. But, John, he asked, 'Does Jesus live here?' And that is different, John!"

Today in America we have our finely expressed creeds, our majestic expressions of worship, our stately churches, and our lovely chapels, and our efficient ecclesiastical systems, but there is a deeper and more searching question which is being asked of you and me as individuals as we tend and cultivate these outer courtyards of the spirit.

Men want to know if God lives in us. On the answer to this question, which we make with our living, may turn the destiny of our nation and the future of mankind. For only through men regenerated by the power of Jesus Christ, who demonstrate His way of life day by day, who are loyally dedicated to God and to country, can America be redeemed for God and for the rôle which she must play in the history now being made.

~~~~~~

CHAPTER IX

Washington, Symbol of the Awakening

Not long ago I climbed the slopes of the Mount of Olives. Reaching its summit, I remembered that here our Lord held His last conference with His disciples. I knelt reverently to touch the ground where He last stood on this earth.

It was late afternoon and, yonder across the Kedron Valley, the glow of a setting sun was spread on the ancient Holy City. Her domes, minarets and spires were silhouetted against a skyline—first crimson, then purple, then gray. Jerusalem lay silent in the afterglow of a brilliant day.

Standing there, I remembered how Jesus looked down on that city and wept. His heart yearned with a mighty compassion for Jerusalem; like all devout and patriotic Jews, Jesus longed to see His people live in complete fidelity to the highest standards they had known. With intimations that this might be His last visit, He cried out in anguished spirit: "O Jerusalem, Jerusalem, thou that killest the prophets, and stonest them which are sent unto thee, how often would I have gathered thy children together, even as a hen gathereth her chickens under her wings, and ye would not."

He sorrowed over the *whole* city—even over the scribes and the Pharisees, whose hypocrisies He had just condemned. With compassion, His plea encompassed them all: the deceived and the deceivers, the poor and the rich, the rulers and the ruled, the plotters and the plunderers, the lowly and the lofty. Again and again He would have gathered the multitudes of this city into His little flock, into the bosom of His beloved fellowship. He would not command or coerce; His was a call of love. Alas for Jerusalem! She would not accept His invitation.

So in His departing words He said, "Your house is left unto you desolate." The city was no longer what once it had been—the seat of God's power and influence. For many years it had been without the Ark, without the Shekinah. Now, rejecting Christ, it was without God's favor. It was left to them, desolate. In the end the renunciation of God's ways led to national ruin. Jerusalem, once the center of religious piety and patriotic devotion, no longer had ears to hear, nor eyes to see, nor heart to respond to God's highest truth. Jerusalem, once the glorious symbol of all that was highest and holiest in Jewish tradition, fell in a few years to a foreign enemy and crumbled away from inner decay.

In all the long years since, Jesus must have wept over many another capital city. His lament over Jerusalem symbolizes His lamentation over the capitals of this world which persistently have turned from Him.

What must He think of our fair capital—most beautiful of all American cities, "the shrine of the patriot's devotion," and lately become the pivotal center of world decisions? Does He look on it with smiling approbation or does He see a canker eating at its very soul?

No other place in all the earth is quite like Washington. It is not a city like other cities. No smokestacks disturb its horizons; no factory gates unfold to admit and discharge the multitudes who make American industry tick; no traffic from the world's sea lanes bring to it the trade of foreign shores; no skyscrapers pierce its clouds to house titans of business. There are no mines here, no blast furnaces, no belching chimneys. But big business is conducted here—business big in its import for human destiny. Its single business is the business of government—the government of the United States of America.

The people who reside in Washington have been sent here by their fellow countrymen: farmers, scholars, merchants, professional folk, men and women from the vast expanse that is America. Others have been drawn here by the requirements of an age of big and powerful government. This capital is a projection of all the cities, towns,

153

hamlets, and countryside which combine to make the United States of America. Every citizen shares in its virtues and vices, in its successes and failures, in its triumphs and trials, its honor and dishonor, its prestige and its responsibilities. America's ideals, standards, spiritual power and character combine to form a cultural mosaic known as Washington. In its complex character, the city is a microcosm of the United States.

Washington is not a city in the civic sense. Almost no one who lives here calls it "my town" in the same sense in which he refers to the town from which he came. But while few call it "home," nearly a million people dwell here—some for a month, some for sixty years. The chances are that whether a man stays one year or fifty, he still refers to another spot as "home" as the place where he votes, to which he attaches great sentiment, and to which he plans some day to return.

If its inhabitants cannot say, "This is my town," they can say something better—something that can be said by every American: "This is my capital—my Washington."

Some time ago considerable interest was aroused by a book called: *Washington Confidential*, which purported to portray the real life of Washington. The authors of this book quite candidly admitted at the outset that their purpose in assembling the material was to satisfy what they believed to be America's appetite for reading. They stated baldly: "We will limit this to what we think will interest you. . . . We have nothing to sell but books. . . . The kind of place we found furnished us with that sole commodity in which we deal—copy."

The authors, Jack Lait and Lee Mortimer, thus frankly admitted they had no passion whatever for reform, no eagerness for remodeling society, no zeal for personal or national redemption—only "copy." If you have read any of their "confidential" material, you must give them credit for achieving their objectives with startling success. With great zeal they seized on moral turpitude, real or supposed; with a scent for scum they served up a sordid saga portraying a tattered and tarnished city inhabited by such morally diseased and spiritually degenerated people as to make a sinner weep.

What these pages reveal is, of course, not "confidential" at all, for really confidential copy cannot be garnered in this fashion nor be portrayed in this manner. Only pastors, doctors, judges, and certain other officials are familiar with the confidential characteristics of this city, which dwellers here have in common with all other people. The pastors of this city know all too well the heartaches, frustrations, loneliness, and personal defects which are peculiar to this city. But these confidences are treated with the reverence and dignity which respect for human personality requires.

There are, perhaps, two responses possible to the mood of the times in which we live. First, there may be only a general morbid curiosity about the wickedness of our fellow countrymen, or there may be a more positive response. It may be that at last a slumbering conscience will awaken.

The old-fashioned American morality may not be altogether dead. Perhaps the wide publicity given such a book as that of Mr. Lait and Mr. Mortimer will mean a new alertness to wrongdoing and a fresh sensitiveness to spiritual values.

For good or ill, what such a book points up is the general post-war moral sag which I endeavored to describe in the first chapter of this book—a moral deterioration which has been one of the greatest in our history. That Washington should have been depicted in such debased terms, and that Americans bought and read the book, is most unfortunate. The document gave nothing new to the world. Sin is as old as the human race. The book named only *some* of the sinners—real or supposed—and charted some of the locations in which some of the sinning was alleged to have been done. It overlooked everything else but sin. At the very time when, for our own and for the world's sake, we need to cultivate a strong, patient, determined, morally responsible and spiritually dynamic America, we got, not "confidence," but "confidential"—"Washington Confidential."

What I should like the world to know is a city of wide streets, spacious parks, stately buildings, uplifting churches, and beautiful monuments to America's past greatness—all aglow today with a creative spirituality.

Who is not stirred to his very depths by the sight of this city—however he approaches it, by highway or skyway, by rail or by road? The white dome of the capitol, the slender but sturdy shaft of the Washington Monument, the hallowed monuments to Lincoln and Jefferson—all these stir the heart and kindle the imagination. They are symbols of the best we represent, symbols of that heritage of goodness and greatness which we would preserve for future generations, and reminders to us that our culture and our character as a nation are basically good and sound and worthy of survival.

In the midst of all the tragic recital of national wrong-doing and the exchange of mudslinging in this great city we may miss our great cultural institutions: art galleries, museums, libraries, worthy undergraduate schools, and our universities. Our Supreme Court and our Federal Bureau of Investigation are institutions respected wherever men follow the practice of law. Our great and influential churches and synagogues, with their tremendous vitality throughout the week as well as on Sundays, are to many visitors the most astounding aspect of this city.

Even the Washington newspaper columnists who report and analyze news of more than local interest and certainly suffer no dearth of news to present to their avid readers, find time and take valuable news space to record their observations of a resurgence of religious vitality in the nation's capital. A series of six articles appeared in the *Washington Daily News* under the title, "The New Mood," which was one news writer's attempt to analyze and evaluate the religious climate in which we live today. The *Washington Post* featured a five-column article on the front page of its city section, entitled "Capital Is Becoming Religious Hub," and documented with pictures of the General Secretary of the National Catholic Welfare Conference, the Director of the Washington office of the National Council of Churches, and workers in the office of B'nai Brith. From such centers as these flows an increasing amount of religious news, and to them come important religious groups for meetings: student groups and visitors from all parts of the world.

Similar articles to these by Robert Tate Allen and Kenneth Dole have appeared in the *Times Herald* and the *Evening Star*. My own files show that excerpts from my sermons and prayers appear in widely separated newspapers. A perusal of the *Congressional Record* would indicate that hardly a day passes but that a senator or congressman puts into the *Record* some religious feature which he deems to have national significance or to contain a message from which the members of the Congress could profit. Some of the material is rich and profound, some of it less penetrating and sometimes superficial, but the fact that it is placed in the official records of the Congress of the United States indicates both that the men and women who serve in the legislative body are for the most part religious people and that they believe that Americans in general are interested in a spiritual way of life.

Seminars, composed of laymen and ministers under denominational auspices as well as under the sponsorship of the National Council of Churches, spend extensive periods several times a year conferring with leaders of government concerning the relationship of religion to the well-being of our people.

There are White House Conferences on Child Welfare, the Physically Handicapped, Education, Old Age, etc., which, while convened under secular auspices, have definite religious connotations.

Several years ago a unique recognition of the spiritual foundations of American democracy found expression in the inauguration of the Annual Washington Pilgrimage of American Churchmen. For a number of years now several hundred churchmen and churchwomen from various sections of the country have devoted three or four days each year to visiting the national shrines symbolic of the faith which has made us great. Visits have been made to the Senate, to the House of Representatives, to the Supreme Court, and to the White House. At each monument and building competent spokesmen (including the President and Vice-President, Justices of the Supreme Court, legislators, diplomats, and clergymen) have interpreted them in terms of the spiritual significance of the national aspirations which brought them into being. At the annual banquet of this Pilgrimage one clergyman and one layman who have contributed to the revival of America's religious spirit are designated clergyman and layman of the year, respectively, and citations are awarded them. The Pilgrimage is appropriately concluded when its members participate in a Sunday service in church where the mood and accent are consonant with the pilgrimage purpose.

So successful was the first Pilgrimage that men and

women from across the nation voluntarily formed a Pilgrimage Corporation, thus assuring the perpetuation and multiplication of its activity. Thus a movement, sparked by an imaginative team—Dr. and Mrs. Harold Dudley —and implemented since by Dr. William A. Leach, editor of *Church Management*, and David C. Cook, Jr., a publisher, has become a meaningful movement which will bless coming generations. After all, why should not Americans of deep faith renew both their Christian and patriotic devotion around the monuments and symbols which proclaim that the course of our being and the guide of our lives is God?

More recently, two concerned clergymen and one layman incorporated a Foundation for Religious Action. Its program will be twofold: first, it will convene annually in Washington a carefully selected group of religious leaders and representatives of government to assess the moral and spiritual climate of the times and to indicate how the resources of religion may be brought to bear on the maintenance of our spiritual foundations. Secondly, recognizing that there is an inadequate positive expression of America's true faith as derived from her religous sources, the Foundation will strive to launch a spiritual offensive through mass communication media in order to supplement or even transcend the efforts of the Government in this field.

A directory of church headquarters and national agencies now functioning in Washington would be a notable document for one who would get the feel of Washington's religious mood. The National Council of Churches has an important segment of its main headquarters here and has assigned to it one of its ablest church statesmen, Dr. Earl F. Adams. The National Catholic Welfare Conference, staffed by 199 workers, unifies, co-ordinates and organizes the Catholic people in works of a varied character. Actually it is the organization of the Roman Catholic Bishops of the United States. Its eight departments, executive, education, press, social action, legal, immigration, youth, and lay, form a clearing house through which the bishop's policies are executed. B'nai Brith, the largest Jewish service organization in the country, has its international headquarters here. In near-by Tacoma Park is located the World Headquarters of the Seventh Day Adventist Church. Here a staff of 250 persons serve the Adventist General Conference, while its Review and Herald Publishing Association employs two hundred more. At the same location is found the Washington Missionary College with an enrollment of 660, and the Adventist Theological Seminary with more than one hundred students.

Sixteen denominations in Washington have national churches which in some official way represent their specific denominations. One of the most beautiful of all houses of worship is the new Washington Mosque, which already is frequently visited by tourists. This institution ministers to Moslems who are in Washington on diplomatic missions, and maintains an Islamic Institute where lectures and seminars are open to the public.

The Church's concern for its ministry to its young

parishioners in the military service is expressed in the very beautiful building of the General Commission on Chaplains, located directly opposite the Supreme Court. This organization acts as a liaison between the Government and some thirty or forty religious organizations throughout the country. In addition to this, many of the churches maintain their own chaplain and service personnel agencies. All over the city hospitality and service centers are being operated in connection with parish churches.

Following his successful evangelistic campaign several years ago, Dr. Billy Graham established his enterprising Evangelistic Film Service in a Connecticut Avenue building, which distributes religious motion pictures to churches throughout the country.

The influence of religion in Washington is also expressed through denominational universities. The Catholic University of America and Georgetown University have long exercised an important influence on the culture of the city. New buildings are being erected on both campuses and, with expanding enrollments, these institutions are likely to be even stronger in the future. Steps are being taken to strengthen the Methodist Church's American University by the erection of new buildings, the establishment of new departments, and the transfer to its Washington campus of the Westminster (Maryland) Theological Seminary. Although today a secular institution, George Washington University, with its enormous student body, still manifests the religious spirit out of which it grew by maintaining a strong department of religion and chaplaincy services.

162

Near by, in Alexandria, is located one of the leading divinity schools of the Protestant Episcopal Church, which for more than a century and a quarter has been preparing clergy for service in that communion.

The Washington Federation of Churches, with 234 member churches, is considered by informed persons to be one of the most effective expressions of co-operative Protestantism in America. Under capable executive leadership, its eight departments, eleven committees and several commissions, co-ordinated by a talented staff, make a tremendous impact on the life of the city. Its department of Research and Church Planning plots the program and assigns responsibilities for the church expansion of participating denominations.

Statistics of church expansion within the greater Washington area indicate that in the period between January, 1947, and November, 1953, 168 Protestant churches were erected or remodeled at a cost of more than $22,000,000. An official of the Roman Catholic Arch Diocese reports that well over $40,000,000 has been invested in seventeen churches, nineteen elementary parochial schools, two high schools, eighteen convents, twenty-one rectories, seventeen auditoriums and sixteen building additions since 1948. New synagogues and religious schools have been erected by seven Hebrew congregations since 1947 at a cost of $4,720,000.

Institutional church life thrives in the nation's capital with a total of approximately 461,000 members of all denominations worshiping in 553 churches and synagogues in the greater Washington area, which comprises Alexandria and Arlington in Virginia, and Prince George and Montgomery counties in Maryland, as well as the District of Columbia.

The fact that only forty per cent of Washington's population appears to belong to Washington churches, while fifty-nine per cent of the nation's population is affiliated with some church, is entirely misleading, since a greater percentage of people in this city than in any other city retain their church membership in churches "back home." On any Sunday of the year, the attendance at services in the church I serve greatly exceeds the communicant membership. This phenomenon, at a time when the average attendance per Sunday throughout the nation is one-third the communicant roll, suggests that religion is a dominant factor in the life of the people of this city.

Latest statistics indicate that Roman Catholics comprise eleven to twelve per cent of the Washington area population; Jews, three and a half to four per cent; and Protestants many times the combined memberships of these other two major faiths.

These reports, impressive as they are, do not tell the full story. Washington is a praying city. From the White House to the Capitol, from the Capitol to the Supreme Court, from the Supreme Court across the Potomac to the Pentagon and around the periphery of the city to the sprawling annexes, from the highest executive to the lowliest clerk can be found hosts of men and women who practice daily prayer and who carry the presence of God with them into their varied vocations. The Senate and House of Representatives not only have chaplains, but these dedicated men pray with and for Senators and Congressmen and render innumerable personal pastoral services.

The International Christian Leadership organization, of which Lt. Gen. Willard S. Paul is president, sponsors fourteen weekly prayer groups within the Washington area. There is a prayer group for senators, another for congressmen, another for the executives, and another for the judiciary, and there are several additional groups related to this movement. Committed and disciplined men and women in the service of the United States government honor God and practice spiritual disciplines. A number of these busy men and women, who are frequently required away from the capital, nevertheless find ways to teach church-school classes, lead devotional services, and serve on church boards. Many of them deliberately schedule periods of time for attendance at church conventions and religious retreats.

Recently I participated in an unforgettable experience of Christian fellowship. Early in the morning, six hundred people—almost entirely laymen—assembled in the main ballroom of the Mayflower Hotel. About small tables sat men and women from many nations whose imposing titles and responsibilities of office were almost forgotten in the simplicity and richness of the fellowship. At the head table sat a half dozen men who participated in the simple program. Charles E. Bennett, a disabled veteran and member of Congress from Florida, offered a heartfelt thanksgiving and blessing for the food. The group breakfasted in quiet fellowship, after which Senator Alexander Wiley read without comment the first Psalm. When he was seated, Vice-President Nixon read: "I am the vine; ye are the branches. He that abideth in me, and I in him, the same bringeth forth much fruit; for without me ye can do nothing. . . . If ye keep my commandments, ye shall abide in my love, even as I have kept my Father's commandments and abide in His love. . . . Ye are my friends if ye do whatsoever I command you."

Beside Senator Frank Carlson of Kansas, who presided, sat President Eisenhower who, at a previous breakfast, had given public testimony to the power of prayer in his own life. Senator Carlson presented the host, Mr. Conrad N. Hilton, who said in his own sincere way:

What I like about prayer is that it is a means of direct communication with God. You can speak to Him any time, night or day, and you can know with certainty that He is listening to you. . . . You can thank Him for the things He has done for you. You can tell Him you are baffled, bewildered, discouraged, or that you are the happiest person in the world. . . . It took a war to put prayer at the center of the lives of our fighting men. It took a war, and the frightening evil of Communism, to show the world that this whole business of prayer is not a sissy, a counterfeit thing that man can do or not as he wishes. Prayer . . . is a part of man's personality, without which he limps. . . . It is with this limp that man walks without God. That is how men grope in darkness unless they believe that God, in his kindness, is willing to lift the shadows if we ask Him in prayer: is willing to raise men to the vision of the children of God if men ask Him in prayer; is willing to help us live like children of God with the permanent peace, and happiness of the children of God—if we ask Him in prayer.

This was no mystic's or theologian's declaration; it was a layman's testimony ringing with reality.

Then the Chief Justice of the United States, Earl Warren, spoke of how, despite the separation of the institutions of religion from the institution of government, there had never been any separation of religion from the life of the nation—that, indeed, from the very beginning we had declared that our national existence was derived from God, that our creation and our dignity as individuals are the gifts of God, and that our ultimate destiny, both as a people and as individuals, is in His hands. He went on to show what the Christian faith had meant in his own life.

The moving occasion was fittingly brought to conclusion in prayer by Abraham Vereide, the man whom God had used to launch this international prayer group movement.

This occasion was not an uncommon one in our capital city; it was simply a somewhat augmented, regularly scheduled breakfast prayer group. Just as this morning there were present the mayor of a German city, a baroness from Sweden, a psychiatrist from Paris, a labor leader from San Francisco, a member of the Canadian Parliament so at every such breakfast can be found men and women from many nations in prayer with fellow Christians.

If my own calendar is any barometer of the spiritual life of this city in which I minister, then Washington is one of the most religious cities in all the world, for my schedule has me leading others in devotions several times a day almost every day in the week—in conferences and conventions and forums ranging from the D. A. R. Congress and the Billy Graham Evangelistic Crusade to the meeting of the Church Federation and the graduation services of the F. B. I. Academy. Such a prayer meeting is not merely a performance to honor an occasion and invest it with respectability, but rather an opportunity to honor God and to draw on His resources.

Think of what happens on the day Congress reconvenes each year. Since 1948, at eight o'clock in the morning of that day, members of the Senate and the House of Representatives have joined with the President and his Cabinet, the Judiciary, and many others in a simple but moving forty-minute service of intercessory prayer and Holy Communion. There is no preaching—only prayer and the sermon in the sacrament. President Truman attended the first such service, and each one thereafter while he was in the White House. President Eisenhower has continued the practice, and was joined in the last service by the Vice-President, the Chief Justice, several Associate Justices of the Supreme Court, most of the Cabinet, hosts of Senators, Congressmen, and other officials. The Moderator of the Presbyterian Church in the U.S.A. presided and among the elders administering the sacrament of Holy Communion were Senators and Congressmen who are ruling elders in their home churches. Although held under Presbyterian auspices, an invitation is always extended to Christians of any communion who desire to participate in the service. From this atmosphere of spiritual reality, men who bear the responsibilities of government go to take up their duties in White House, Supreme Court, and the new sessions of the Congress. Nobody present in such a service comes away without an inner assurance that these men are possessed of greater power because they have paused that day in God's house.

Nothing is quite so inspiring to me as Washington on a Sunday morning. The streets are empty of shoppers and bustling workers, but they are alive with human traffic en route to church. This religious spirit manifested itself not just last year or year before last or the year before that. In varying degrees, Washington always has been a religious city. Now the spirit is both more intensive and more inclusive than ever before. Today the city is charged with spiritual vitality. Americans talk about it; foreigners comment on the amazing phenomenon; tourists are touched by it, and commentators attempt to analyze it. Everyone observes, feels, and absorbs some of it. The religious climate is infectious and transmissive. It is not merely formal, nor is it superficial; it is genuine and sincere. It has the essence of reality.

On busy Connecticut Avenue—just in front of the National Presbyterian Church—stands an imposing statue of John Witherspoon, Colonial revolutionary and patriot and the only clergyman to sign the Declaration of Independence. Fittingly enough, the monument was erected, not by the church, but by the Congress of the United States, in recognition of his contribution to the ideological substance and meaning of the American Revolution. With his Bible clasped firmly in his right hand, he is shedding his pulpit gown and stepping out of God's house into the councils of men to take his place in their common life.

Today many a man—like Witherspoon—is drinking at the wells of spiritual life in the sanctuaries of God to strengthen himself with God's word and His living truth and to sustain himself in the life of today's America.

This is the real Washington. This is my Washington— the symbol of America's great spiritual renaissance.

~~~~~~

CHAPTER X

A Summons to Americans

On top of a mountain in Cape Breton, Nova Scotia, where these lines are being written, rests all that is mortal of Alexander Graham Bell. Dr. Bell named this mountain Beinn Bhreagh, which is the Gaelic for "Beautiful Mountain." Here at his summer home, atop the mountain which projects itself into the heart of the Bras d'Or Lakes, and surrounded by scenes reminiscent to him of the highlands of the old country, Bell received many of his most creative insights. Frequently he walked to the top of the mountain, from which the panorama of lake and highlands spread out beneath him, to stimulate his fertile imagination. Sometimes he walked over the slopes of Beinn Bhreagh in torrents of rain, when electrical storms illuminating the skies seemed to fire his spirit. The very summit of the mountain was a favorite rendezvous for Dr. Bell and his wife, Mabel Hubbard Bell. So fond were they of this peak that Dr.

Bell directed that on his death he should be interred there.

Visitors today to the crest of this mountain find a huge natural boulder on which is secured a bronze tablet with the following inscription:

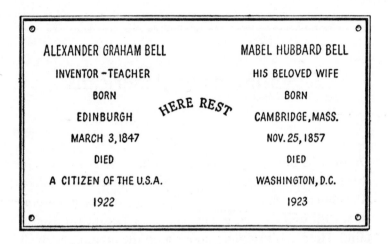

ALEXANDER GRAHAM BELL	MABEL HUBBARD BELL
INVENTOR –TEACHER	HIS BELOVED WIFE
BORN	BORN
EDINBURGH	CAMBRIDGE, MASS.
MARCH 3, 1847	NOV. 25, 1857
DIED	DIED
A CITIZEN OF THE U.S.A.	WASHINGTON, D.C.
1922	1923

HERE REST

"A citizen of the U. S. A."! Bell's story was long and great. His epitaph might have recited the record of his numerous inventions and the honors which mankind had bestowed upon him in gratitude for his services. But he asked that what he cherished most be written over his grave, the fact that he was *A citizen of the United States.*

How glibly many of us accept the privilege which belongs to us as citizens of the United States! How few of us ever pause to evaluate our citizenship or our form of government. What is it that distinguishes our kind of life? What are the salient features of our democratic form of government?

172

Our kind of democracy is based on a high faith in the capacity of the common man, and that means most of us; it is based on faith in his spiritual capacity, in his ability to discern the truth, accept the truth, and live by the truth, and in his capacity to see and accept and live by high democratic ideals.

Our kind of democracy is based on the belief that man as an individual is of highest value in all the universe and that he is possessed of a high moral dignity because of his relation to his Creator. Because he is created in the image of God, and because his dignity is not his own achievement but the bestowal of the Creator, whatever hurts his personality is evil and whatever enhances his personality is good. Freedom itself is not an achievement, but the gift of God; and no dictator or state has the right to take from man the freedom he possesses as the creature of the Creator. Man, blemished by sin as he is, *can* be redeemed and remodeled and made the instrument for God's will on earth.

Our kind of democracy believes that man, with such lofty spiritual origins and capacities, can be led to put the general good above his own selfish interests and ambitions, and that he can find his truest happiness in service.

Our kind of democracy is based on belief in freedom of speech and assembly and press, though we realize that many foolish things and some untrue things may be said in our political strivings and quarrels.

Our kind of democracy is based on belief that the will of the people—the will of men with high dignity and moral purpose—is to be expressed through the ballot. Are we awake to our civic responsibility as Christians? Grandfather

173

did a much better job here than we are doing. In 1896, out of every 100 voters, 83 were at the polls, although there was then no easy transportation to help an individual from his place of business to the ballot box. Twenty years later, in the Presidential election of 1916, the figure had dropped to 72 out of every 100 persons. In another twenty years—by 1936—the figure dropped to 60 out of every 100 who exercised their responsibility. Only twelve years later, in the election of 1948, barely 50 out of every 100 potential American voters cast their ballots. Eighty-three per cent—72 per cent—and now 50 per cent—until today hundreds of thousands of persons have not even registered to vote. If we drift into minority control of government, it is our own fault. If good citizens do not vote and vote wisely, bad men can assume that good people do not care. "All that is necessary for the triumph of evil," said Edmund Burke, "is that good men do nothing." Going to the polls, thinking, studying, and evaluating issues and candidates, this, in our kind of democracy, should be as sacred a duty as going to church.

Where do all these concepts come from? While it is true that many historic movements contributed to the origin and development of our democratic life, it is a simple fact of history that our ideals and standards are derived largely from the Judaic-Christian tradition. And to an extent sometimes not fully appreciated America is the logical culmination of the Protestant Reformation.

Democracy as we know it in America is so much a child of the Christian religion that there is no reason to suppose

174

that where Christ has ceased to grip and inspire men the foundation of democracy can be maintained. Let us be honest! Our kind of democracy depends on religion. It depends on the Christian religion. Its ideas are Christian ideas. Its ideals are Christian ideals. Its goals are Christian goals. Allow Christian faith and practice to languish, and democracy as we know it begins to disintegrate.

If democracy should ever vanish in this land it will be because we are not sufficiently Christian. We cannot play at religion and trifle with our inheritance and keep the American way. We deserve it only in proportion to our willingness to cultivate the qualities of character worthy of it.

In his last public address Woodrow Wilson, "The Road Away from Revolution," said:

The sum of the whole matter is this, that our civilization cannot survive materially unless it is redeemed spiritually. It can be saved only by becoming permeated with the spirit of Christ, and being made free and happy by the practices which spring out of that spirit. Only thus can discontent be driven out and all the shadows lifted from the road ahead.

Here is the final challenge to our churches, to our political organizations, and to our capitalists—to everyone who fears God or loves his country. Shall we not all earnestly co-operate to bring in the new day?

How much we need to realize the importance of personal loyalty to our faith! Is it not true that the man who neglects his faith, who absents himself from his church, who fails to read his Bible, who does not pray, who does

175

not seek to discover the will of God for his life is a menace and a peril to our democracy? On the other hand, is not every citizen who cultivates his inner life, who worships God Almighty, who is disciplined by prayer and Christian fellowship, who is committed to and teaches Christian morality, who maintains a Christian home and takes seriously his responsibility to society—is he not, however humbly, building the foundation on which our democracy depends?

Do we deserve democracy? That nation deserves democracy "whose God is the Lord." Our kind of democracy is possible only when people are committed to principles of human dignity and the value of human personality, of faith and trust in one another, and when they have an invincible faith in the presiding providence of God. Only where a large segment of people are dedicated to Christ and His Church can our kind of democracy succeed.

There are more laudable and certainly more basic reasons for joining the church than that of patriotism. But certainly, in this kind of world and in our kind of democracy, one of the most patriotic things a man can do is to join a church in the tradition of the emancipated spirit and to work at his religion.

Do we deserve democracy? We deserve it only if we take seriously our responsibility to pray, to think, to work for the Kingdom of God; only if we really have faith in human individuals as did our fathers; only if we are the kind of men and women who can be trusted with their own destiny; only if we have the courage to establish economic

176

well-being and social justice; only if we contribute to the
making of a moral peace between the nations; only if we
cultivate day by day those interior resources which make
us truly Christian; only if the church is really the
church— "the redeemed of the Lord—the salt of the
earth—a colony of heaven."

Do we deserve democracy? Only when we live by great
convictions! America was founded by men of great convictions, and no one can understand America today without recognizing that many of us have lost those convictions about God and man and democratic processes. When
convictions are lost, a generation grows up without moral
moorings. Without moral moorings, bad convictions often
displace good convictions. Godless men are inclined to
substitute the worship of the state for the worship of the
eternal and almighty God. The only power which can
overcome bad convictions is the recovery of good convictions. The paradox of this post-war world is that on the
one hand we have been participants and spectators in a
great moral sag and cultural deterioration and, on the
other, that we are being swept along by the tides of a great
religious renaissance. Will the religious awakening be
deep and thoroughgoing enough to make us sufficiently
great and good and strong for the redemption of the world?
Will we achieve the recovery of our great convictions?

The back-to-church movement is laudable and it is necessary, but it is not sufficient in itself. It is not enough to be
part of the Church if it is to be only a social gesture, like
joining the Chamber of Commerce or the Country Club.

177

If the trek back to church is simply another manifestation of mass man's influence over individual man, or a way of adjusting to the current climate and trend, it will end in futility. If it is merely the operation of the law of conformity and adjustment, it cannot be the dynamic force we need in this hour.

Christianity is more than social adjustment. Christianity is more than conformity to the community. Christianity is more than blending into the community of which one is a part, no matter how good that community may be. Christianity is more than synchronizing one's life with the forces which play on it. Christianity is commitment to Jesus Christ. To be a Christian is to be a forgiven, redeemed, cleansed, remodeled and reinforced person through the power of Jesus Christ working in individual personality. There must be a depth of devotion, a penetration of insight, and an ultimate and complete commitment to Jesus Christ, who by transforming its citizens redeems the nation.

Nor is it enough to find in the Church simply a refuge from worry and fear and anxiety, or a boon to better business, or an expansion of personal friendships. The Church is "the beloved community." It is the society of the redeemed. Its purpose is to change the whole life of the individual and in so doing to influence the total life of men—or it is not the Church.

A tepid Church and a half-hearted people can never stand up to the demands of this age. There are demonic forces at work. "We wrestle not against flesh and blood,

178

but against principalities, against powers, against the rulers of the darkness of this world, against spiritual wickedness in high places."

I shall never forget an experience which I had one summer day some years before World War II, in a well-known city in Southern Russia. I left my modest hotel at daybreak and wandered unescorted through the streets of the old city, past the scaffolding of partially completed buildings and shops yet unvisited, occasionally meeting a forlorn dog or a solitary peasant, until I came at last to a great church. At least it appeared to be a great church. Approaching the massive structure, I was confronted at the main entrance by two guards with rifles and fixed bayonets. Since I was obviously not a thief and promptly produced my "intourist" identification book, the guards reluctantly admitted me.

Inside, the altar and reredos were gone. Tapestry and tinsel were no longer visible. The gaudy accoutrements of worship, so familiar in the Eastern Church, had been desecrated, and a musty smell had displaced the aroma of incense and candle smoke. Only the shell of a house of worship remained.

Instead of functioning as a church, the entire building had become a granary. A pile of threshed wheat was heaped on the floor in the form of an inverted cone, its base covering the entire cathedral area and its point reaching far up into the dome. The early morning sun poured through stained glass windows, and its multicolored rays played weirdly on the pile of wheat. Figures of saints and martyrs flashed in the remnants of the windows. Above, around the interior of the dome, was a dim but beautiful mural of our Lord breaking bread with His disciples on the night which was the night of the Institution and also of His betrayal.

Alone with my thoughts, I could understand how often our Lord must have looked down on that Church—remote from the people, aloof from man's common need, unresponsive to the forces about it, now identified with an insensitive and inept ruler, giving tacit consent to its tyranny. That church was only the shell that desecration had made it; and the judgment of God was on it.

What a warning! A church no longer relevant to life is crushed. But the church which is faithful in its witness and relevant to the life about it will live and lift the culture in which it is set. When true to its Lord, neither secularism, nor materialism, nor "the gates of hell itself" can prevail against it.

The old-fashioned frontier has gone. Our frontier now is both nearer in time and distance and yet farther away in its lack of neighborliness, understanding, and co-operation. What the wilderness was to our ancestors, the skies above us and the waters of the sea are to us today. For many years to come we shall not be certain what evil tidings and what terrible dangers they may bear. It is going to take great character to measure up to the demands of the future. In all the contests of the present and coming age we must be morally resolute and spiritually powerful. Above all else, we must not lose the struggle for the souls

180

of men at home and we must not lose the campaign for men's souls abroad.

There are many foreigners, and not a few Americans, who never really comprehend this newcomer among the nations. Our power and wealth and prosperity, which we are so fond of displaying did not come by accident, nor are they merely the normal result of vast natural resources and spacious lands. What the world does not always understand is that this outward physical expression of our riches and strength is the result of an audacious, creative spirit emanating from a great faith.

A discerning observer from abroad who really knows us comprehends this truth. The Lebanese Ambassador, Dr. Charles Malik, in an address before the Washington Federation of Churches, pointed this out clearly:

The United States is new to the world scene. It suddenly finds itself able to wield unprecedented power. It is natural, therefore, for some people who do not fully know you to be afraid of you: they feel you are not sufficiently seasoned in the exercise of power. They do not know that there are in the classical American character wonderful reserves of humanity, humility and humor, and that in the fundamental accent upon the dignity of the individual and his worth you have a real salvation from the possible abuse of power.

This means that in the exercise of your leadership, others, no matter how weak or small, must be taken as real partners. . . . Partnership means sharing on every level of human existence, each with his own means and according to his own light. A partnership that shares only the external husks of life, leaving the inner springs of the spirit hidden and unreleased, will soon pale off into boredom and unreality. The

world rightly expects the revelation of what America ultimately really believes in. Nothing is more needful today than
the adequate articulation of this message. . . . It requires the
greatest possible sense of responsibility to truth, to God and
to history. What is needed, therefore, is for scholars, philosophers, poets and saints to bear upon the determination of
history. I pray for the active presence of philosophy, poetry,
and God in the capitals of the world. Then the weight of
America will be informed and sustained, not only with politics
and power, but with truth, with vision, and with holiness.

Dr. Malik is right. Americans, when true to themselves,
can never get very far away from God. The life of this
republic was cradled in the faith that God presides over
His universe and that nations and men in the end are
accountable to Him. By His act this nation came into being
and in His spirit it has become great among the peoples of
the earth. This does not mean that we are a political pet
of the Almighty. It does mean that because of our faith
Americans have an obligation to exalt and to glorify God.
It is only when we cease to worship and to pray, when we
ignore God's wisdom and truth, that we become sick ourselves and are misunderstood by others. That is why today's
religious renaissance is the most important aspect of our
age. That is why the rôle of the Church is more important
today than at any time in human history.

Many Americans are concerned today about what they
call "security," but what is security? Are we really achieving
it? These are questions of real moment which we do well
to raise.

Some time ago I was dining with two men on a train,

en route to New York. One was an engineer, the other a chemist. They were civilians representing a great industry that was working with our military services in the development of our new ingenious weapons, about which most of us have only scant information. Said one of these scientists: "I don't know everything concerning these developments, but I know enough to feel secure in the knowledge that if war should come today we could successfully end it tomorrow afternoon."

Did that man have real security?

Here is another man in his mid-forties, who has provided health insurance, disability insurance, unemployment insurance, life insurance, education insurance, and all the rest of it for himself and his family, but when he went to his doctor he learned that he was afflicted with ulcers as a result of persistent anxiety. His psychiatrist said he had a depressive psychosis as a result of his outlook on the future of his family and the world.

With all the provisions he had made, this man was dying of insecurity.

Look at the early Christians. Let the pages of the New Testament give their testimony. The people in whom our faith was born, and in whose lives it became incandescent, had no insurance system, no pension system, no social security programs and certainly no assurance of protection against hostile forces. Some of them were poor and some of them were prosperous. They came from varied classes and positions in the social structure. They lived at a time when it appeared the world might go to pieces—when, as a

183

matter of fact, the Roman Empire, greatest empire of old, did completely disintegrate. Yet these people had security. They had purity of life and a moral correctness from which they would not deviate. They believed that the universe itself supported their way of life. There was a permanence in their family relationships which gave them a firmness and steadfastness which the pagan world did not have. Moreover, there was a solidarity about the larger family found in the fellowship of the Church. And to this sense of family and community solidarity was added a persistent faith in eternal principles and values. They were certain that the way of Christ was correct, that in the end Jesus Christ—His Gospel and His Kingdom—would triumph. God was at the center of the universe; through Christ they had come to know God. They staked everything on that faith. Peter wrote, "Who is he that will harm you, if ye be followers of that which is good?"

They followed good as they found it in their Lord Jesus Christ. They were persecuted, tormented, and sometimes were killed, but they sang a song of triumph amid suffering and death. They had "security," but it was the security of perfect faith, not what we are inclined to call security. They faced uncertain crops. They lived under a primitive economy. And they were always in mortal peril of their neighbors. Yet they endured, knowing that they had the assurance of heaven.

It was not a minister, but the man who is now Secretary of State who wrote in 1951: "Something has gone wrong with us, or we should not be in our present plight and mood. It is not like us to be on the defensive and to be fearful. This is new in our history. What we lack is a righteous and dynamic faith. Without it, all else avails us little. The lack cannot be compensated by politicians, however able; or by scientists, however inventive; or by bombs, however powerful. Our greatest need is to regain confidence in our spiritual heritage." Thus wrote John Foster Dulles.

The truth of the matter is that security depends in the end on spiritual security. Spiritual security is primary, and the source and center of all else; material security is only derivative. How, then, are men to be sustained?

From the Church of Jesus Christ comes the answer. Men will be fearful when they place ultimate reliance on that which is not ultimately reliable; when they put their trust in that which is not ultimately trustworthy. Only God is sufficient, for God only is absolutely reliable and trust-worthy. The antidote to insecurity is in being right with God, in keeping God's laws, in doing God's will, in living in harmony with the moral order of the universe. If we want real security, it is to be found in the only place it ever has been found—in the eternal and living God. Today, as of old, the unyielding truth is this: "Seek ye first the kingdom of God . . ." not *in order that* we may have *things,* but "Seek ye first the kingdom of God . . ." for God's sake, and seek righteousness for the sake of righteousness, and all these *things* shall be added.

Our panaceas and programs may be helpful in alleviating fear-producing situations, and our sociological blueprints and governmental social security programs do tend to minimize the superficial manifestations of insecurity, but real security comes only by being firmly fastened by faith in the eternal God. The psalmist had the secret: "The Lord is the strength of my life, of whom shall I be afraid? . . . He that dwelleth in the secret place of the Most High shall abide under the shadow of the Almighty. . . . I will say of the Lord, He is my refuge and my fortress; my God. In him will I trust."

No lukewarm or easy-going religion will be sufficient for this day. Nor can we expect the pagans to do what must be done in this hour. Only committed men and women can do this. Others, let us hope, will be infused and empowered by contact with those whose souls are rekindled. There is no getting away from it: if we have not yet come to understand that we must return in a very real and earnest way to the basic principles of American life as expressed in evangelical Christianity, then we are not yet aware of the meaning of these days. Only committed men can lead.

One never knows how much influence a single dedicated man can have on other people. I once played football under a great coach. When he read from the Bible and then offered prayers before our class, his simple act (which was reflected in his life and conduct) had more influence on me than any minister I ever met in my boyhood. My father's prayers before he went to bed at night and as soon as he wakened in the morning did something for him; and the sight of him on his knees, despite fatigue and a busy schedule, did something for me. Pagans may dismiss all this

186

with a shrug, but I have to confess that my father and my football coach gained on their knees a sense of righteousness as well as a sense of love and compassion which we could well afford to possess today.

The power of what one committed layman can do in the nation at large is indicated by the example of our President. Of him, the President of the Washington Ministerial Union, Dr. Albert P. Shirkey, has said: "President Eisenhower has resurfaced our religious faith. His spiritual example, as a Presbyterian layman, has made it easier for us clergymen to talk religion to practical-minded laymen. He has popularized prayer and righteousness, so that we now see business and professional men who were once skeptical and cynical about religion joining breakfast prayer meetings and giving up their Sunday golf to join their families in church."

The author of the Book of Chronicles was neither a warrior nor a politician. He was a deeply religious man, summoning his nation to return to the life which once it had known. His call to the people of his day might well echo across our land today: "If my people which are called by my name, shall humble themselves, and pray, and seek my face, and turn from their wicked ways: then will I hear from heaven, and will forgive their sins, and will heal their land."

"If my people, which are called by my name . . ." Who are they? They are the people who believe in God. Under the new Covenant, they are Christian people who seek to know and do His will. If the people of God will take His course, then His resources are available to do the rest.

"If my people will humble themselves . . ." Humility is not one of our national virtues, and it does not come easily for individual Americans. Yet we must be humble. No matter how lofty our position or how insignificant our estate, only the humble man is any good at all in the eyes of God. And no man is so elevated that he cannot look up to the Almighty.

"If my people will pray . . ." If we are too busy to pray, we are too busy. We dare not leave prayer to the spiritual geniuses. This message talks about "my people"—the people called by God's name, Christian folk. That means you, and not the prayer specialist alone.

"If my people will seek my face . . ." God has made us for Himself and when we are most truly ourselves we are channels of His spirit and instruments of His power. If we go humbly to God, and pray as we ought, then He will "make his face to shine upon us." We will be like Him and, being like Him, the results are assured.

This is what will happen: "You will hear from heaven." Sins will be forgiven—those sins which are confessed. And we are not sinless; we have our own guilt in this world. We wanted our soldiers home. We wanted our new homes, our money, our gadgets, our prosperity more than we wanted God and His righteousness. If we confess our sins "we will hear from heaven." We will be forgiven. "If we confess our sins, he is faithful and just to forgive us our sins, and to cleanse us from all unrighteousness." Thank

God, at this hour there are vivid signs that America is alive to moral realities and that a spiritual revival is penetrating the very heart of the nation. Let us pray that it may take dramatic expression and encompass in its sweep the whole of this land.

God has promised the repentant that they "will hear from heaven," that their sins will be forgiven, and that their land will be healed. May this land be encompassed by such a tide of the spirit that our national life may be completely integrated and empowered because it is built on faith in a covenanting God.

Today comes the summons to America: "Blessed is the nation whose God is the Lord . . ."

Lord of our churches,

Lord of our homes,

Lord of our schools,

Lord of our colleges,

Lord of our ballot boxes,

Lord of our Government,

Lord of our peace tables,

Lord of our world.

Let us affirm by our lives that we are a "nation whose God is the Lord."